"*I was rewarded by an intense memory of men whose courage had shown me the power of the human spirit…That spirit which could withstand the utmost assault. Such men had inspired me to be at my best when things were very bad, and they outweighed all the failures. Against the war and its brutal stupidity those men had stood glorified by the thing which sought to destroy them.*"

—*Siegfried Sassoon,*
"WWI Memoirs of an Infantry Officer"
(1930)

"*All the world's a stage,*
And the men and women merely the players."

—*William Shakespeare,*
"As You Like It" *(1623)*

COMMISSIONED IN BATTLE

A Combat Infantryman in the Pacific, WWII

Jay Gruenfeld
with Todd DePastino

To the brave Filipinos who resisted the Japanese occupation and aided American soldiers on Luzon.

And to my late wife Jan, the best thing that has happened to me in a full and largely happy life.

CONTENTS

CHAPTER ONE

Last Day

❦

My last day as an active warrior began in a rain-soaked foxhole on Hill 860 near the Ipo Dam, about twenty-five miles northeast of Manila on the Angat River on Luzon in the Philippines. It was May 15, 1945, the ninth day of the Ipo Dam offensive and my ninetieth as a battlefield commissioned rifle platoon leader in the 103d Infantry Regiment of the 43d Division. I was twenty years and three months old, a veteran of two campaigns and coming to the end of the greatest, most enriching time of my life.

For the past four months and seven days, I'd been in combat on Luzon continuously, except for two several day rests, grabbing a few hours sleep on the ground and bathing out of my helmet

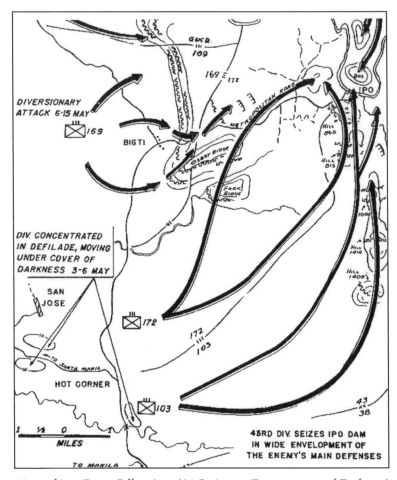

Map of Ipo Dam Offensive. (*U.S. Army, Department of Defense*)

HILL
803   IPO DAM   HILL
860   TO
MT KATITINGA

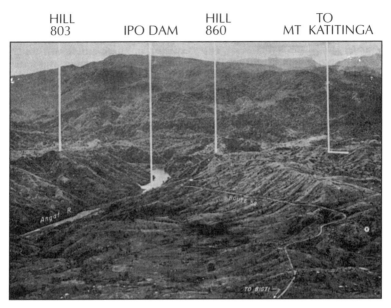

Photograph of Ipo Dam Offensive. (*U.S. Army, Department of Defense*)

when I got the chance. I had, to my knowledge, killed at least fifteen Japanese, some with grenades, but most with my M1 Garand. Some were so close I could have bayoneted them. I prayed daily on Luzon for strength that I might fulfill my duty. A couple times, while under mortar fire, I've broken down and prayed for a Golden Wound that would send me home. By my last day, I knew I probably wouldn't survive the war without a serious wound or sickness. Yet, like so many frontline riflemen, I'd become tough and took pride in enduring what seems unendurable.

Camaraderie made this possible. Together, we laughed in the grimmest of circumstances and devoted ourselves completely to our mission and each other's welfare. I knew of no other bond like it. When, after the war, I read Siegfried Sassoon's remark that his comrades in the trenches of World War I "stood glorified by the thing which sought to destroy them," I understood exactly what he meant.

As platoon leader, I comprehended just enough of our mission this last day to know it was important. We attacked the Ipo Dam to save Manila, which American and Filipino forces had liberated in early March. Cut off from the dam's clean water supply, the city was on the verge of a cholera epidemic. The 43d Division was in the best position to move quickly, so with little preparation or reconnaissance of the area, we found ourselves in this strange mountain terrain, part jungle, part grassland studded with wild outcroppings of rock.

The Japanese, exhausted like us and poorly supplied, occupied a raggedy defensive line between the dam and Manila that tightened into a ring at Hill 860. Nambu machine gun pits, mortars, and artillery hid among the rock slabs, jungle stands, and shallow caves above the dam. Seven thousand entrenched soldiers awaited our approach, about 2,000 more than we anticipated.

On my last day, late in the morning, a Nebraska farm kid turned radioman named Chuck Wakeley relayed a message from our new C-Company commander, Captain Galyea.

"Galyea wants you to send over a squad to help out Mullins' platoon," Wakeley said. "They're in a helluva fight."

I saw Mullins' 3d platoon about 300 to 400 yards east of my position. They were stuck on a steep open ridge. I had only two squads left. Battle wounds and disease had more than halved our original fighting strength of forty-two men. I ran over to my squad leader, Staff Sergeant Hollis Morang, and his assistant Sergeant Harris Choate.

"Take your men and head over to 3d platoon," I ordered. "They need help." Then I added, "I'm coming with you."

I didn't have to join the ten-man squad. According to battlefield procedure—by the book—my job was to stay at platoon HQ, my foxhole, and direct action. But I never considered staying back. Playing the role of fearless leader, despite some fear, was what kept me going. I couldn't surrender the façade.

Soldiers standing upright under fire adopt a characteristic hunch in all wars in all places, as if to make themselves a smaller target, which is what they're instinctively doing. We assumed that position as we made our way east-southeast down Hill 860. The soft ground threw up little splashes of mud where bullets occasionally struck around us, like hail on a muddy road.

The trapped 3d platoon occupied a slope offering little cover, save an occasional tree and ankle high grass that drooped with rain. Machine gun fire prevented their advance, while a large force of Japanese rifleman harassed them from the rear and right. The forward part of the platoon was pinned down in an untenable position, surrounded on three sides.

I arrived to find the rest of the platoon, at least twelve men, with rifles and a machine gun, but they weren't firing. Their closest target was a honey, about twenty Japanese riflemen arranged in columns of two 200 yards to the south, directly downhill from their position.

"Everyone get ready to fire on my count of four!" I shouted.

The blast scattered all twenty Japanese but one. The lone enemy remained in place either dead or too badly wounded to leave.

Almost immediately, the sporadic rifle fire we'd been receiving from the south exploded in intensity. The rounds struck everywhere, and we returned them. Through the rain, I spotted a rifle muzzle showing an unusual amount of flash and smoke. Most Japanese rifles were smokeless and presented little flash. Perhaps it was one of our M1s being used against us. I watch carefully and, after three flashes, determined the location of the shooter. I squeezed off a shot. The muzzle flash ceased.

I looked back at the machine gun, and no one was on it.

"Get someone on that damn gun!" I shouted, adding a generous dose of Army expletives for emphasis.

Then, I took another shot, and my rifle jammed. For the first time in my Army career, I'd not cleaned it after heavy use. The seventy-odd rounds I fired the day before fouled the action. I was in the worst firefight of my war, and I was ineffective. Shit. I struggled with my rifle as Japanese rounds hit so close they splashed mud in my face.

But we had bigger problems than that.

Our mortars and artillery, so helpful against the supply-challenged Japanese on Luzon, were absent. The torrential rains slowed down the whole offensive, transforming our few engineered mountain roads into winding strips of mud. I later learned that our mortar squads had been ordered to save their ammunition until our supply routes could re-open. That left us without the biggest advantage we had against the Japanese: superior firepower.

A voice called out, "Gruenfeld!" I turned to see Captain Galyea in a foxhole not thirty feet from me. Why hasn't he been directing fire? I wondered. He must have been afraid of unleashing the kind of response from the Japanese that we were getting. But this kind of war, a grim war of attrition, wasn't about gaining valuable real estate or seizing commanding ground. It was about killing. You had to kill to take the ground. The enemy seldom retreated.

"Gruenfeld, send a noncom and four men over there to help Mullins," Galyea ordered, pointing uphill to the northeast where the rest of the 3d platoon was located. "They're in trouble."

I relayed the order to Morang, who took off with his men. I wished I'd gone with them.

Just minutes later, Morang returned and dropped into my foxhole. His face had two ugly purple-edged holes in it where a .31 caliber bullet had entered and exited.

"You gotta get over there, Jay," he puffed. "Mullins is hit. Nearly everyone is hit."

I reached down to my pistol belt, grabbed my medicine kit, and tore open a sulfa packet. I held it over Morang's face. My hand trembled involuntarily, distributing the sulfa powder into the ugly holes. So much for being fearless.

After wrapping Morang's head in a bandage, I left the foxhole and headed 150 yards uphill. Reaching the crest, I ran into one of our company's radiomen, my friend Bill Mitchell, staggering out toward our lines. His face was gray and vacant. He's a goner, I thought. Mitch was delivering ammunition to the 3d platoon when a bullet entered the front of his right shoulder and blasted a big hole left of his backbone. It broke a rib and collapsed his lung. Still, I found out later, he refused at first to leave the field. He saw a dead Japanese officer in a foxhole and wanted his saber. With a carbine slung over his only good arm, his left, Mitch stopped in the middle of the firefight and tried for the sword. The carbine slid down his arm and slammed to the ground. Three times Mitch bent over to reach for the prized souvenir before thinking better of it and stumbling over to our medic, Bert Johnson. There was an eyewitness to Mitch's souvenier hunt.

Bert, himself wounded in the shoulder, was now a busy man. After quickly patching up Mitch and sending him back to our company command post, he began working on another bleeding soldier and then another. I crouched a couple yards below him. The side hill was steep with only the grass to protect us from Japanese rifle fire coming mainly from the east. Uphill to the north about 150 yards, I saw two of the 3d platoon's riflemen prone on the ground exposed to this fire. Their officer, Lt. Mullins, has been evacuated, shot in the head. With no artillery or mortar support, their position and ours were untenable. I called for the two prone men to withdraw.

"We have a wounded man here!" one of them yelled back pointing down the hill.

I shifted my eyes below them and spotted the wounded man being dragged in our direction by another soldier.

An exhausted mind doesn't always know it's exhausted, and in combat adrenaline overwhelms the senses. I tried to stay clinical, focused on getting the job done with a minimum of casualties. These prone men appeared to be sitting ducks. I couldn't allow them to be added to our rapidly growing casualty list.

"Get out of there!" I hollered back. "We'll take care of the wounded man!"

I've sometimes wondered since if that order was a mistake.

Another gray-faced soldier, caked in mud, lurched toward me. It was Joe Briones, one of our scouts, a replacement, and the wag who christened our 2d platoon "The Fighting Deuce." Joe had always kept us in good humor during the worst of times, and I counted him a special friend.

"Hi, Joe," I said nonchalantly as he flopped next to me in obvious shock.

He'd been shot through his elbow and other places and was bleeding badly. Bert our medic was working on someone else, so I did what I could for Joe, which wasn't much. I put his arm in a sling and bandaged some holes as he slipped out of consciousness. Then, I laid him down and said goodbye. He was probably already dead when I rose and headed out to help the wounded man on the hill.

Before leaving, I briefly considered staying back with Joe. Going out would attract more fire, since adding a third man to a pair makes for a more attractive target. But, I reasoned, we'd all stand a better chance of surviving once we got that wounded man out of there since two crawling men made good enough targets in low grass. Besides, I didn't feel right remaining in the relative safety of my position while a fallen soldier and his rescuer lay vulnerable on the battlefield. It went against my role, and my role was everything to me.

I ran 150 yards in wet grass like a man hurrying home in a rainstorm. Bullets splashed about, revealing just how many guns were trained on our position. But they were a couple hundred yards away, too far, in rain at least, to get the job of hitting me done without a great many shots.

I bent down to the wounded man from the 3d platoon. It's Pedro. I knew him slightly. I was surprised to find he recognized me though I was caked in mud, wore no insignia, and toted an M-1 Garand instead of a carbine, which most lieutenants carried.

Dragging Pedro was my friend Brum, Virgil Brumfield, a superb replacement who was Joe Briones' scouting partner.

"We'll get you out, Pedro," I said.

"I know you will, Lieutenant," he replied.

We were both wrong.

I all but threw my rifle to Brum and crouched down next to Pedro to put him in a fireman's carry across my shoulders. I reached for his left wrist. Part of his hand was missing, and the wrist was smashed. So rather than gripping his forearm, I mistakenly wrestled his 170 pound body on to my left shoulder and staggered off balance across the steep slope. After several steps I slipped, and both of us crashed into the mud. Pedro groaned. Brum helped to position Pedro on my back for a second try. As I was about to raise him up, I heard a sharp crack and my right arm went dead. A .31 caliber bullet had entered and exited just above the elbow, cutting clear through my bicep and severing nerves.

"I'm hit, Brum," I grunted.

"Then get the hell out of here!" Brum replied.

I pressed my left thumb against the artery in my arm and hustled my way back to Bert. I added to his growing backlog of cases on the hillside. He grabbed my arm and pulled out a knife to cut away my sleeve. All of a sudden, what felt like a bolt of lightening surged through my body.

The jolt of electricity knocked me into a black void. I tumbled into darkness, and time seemed to stop. I entered a serene twilight state of unemotional detachment.

"So this is the way it feels to die," I said to myself. Then, before I even hit the ground, more spontaneous words formed in my mind:

I believe in God, the Father Almighty, maker of Heaven and Earth…

Before starting the second line of the Apostles' Creed, I re-gained consciousness. Bert, who had seen my eyes roll back in my head, asked, "What's the matter?"

"I'm hit low," I responded, looking down at my legs. They moved, but I couldn't feel them.

Bert examined the holes where a .25 caliber bullet had entered my left hip and exited my right.

"You're lucky," deadpanned Bert, who administered morphine and began patching me up. "It just grazed you."

In my case, there was some truth to this old

well-meaning lie. If that bullet had been .31 caliber, it would have severed my spine, but the lighter .25 caliber jogged around it and saved my legs.

I was numb but perfectly alert, lying in the rain next to Bert, Joe Briones, who was dead, and another dead soldier Bert couldn't save. With no rifle and only one arm, I felt vulnerable and wondered briefly what I'd do if the Japanese attacked us. But I quickly resigned myself to being a spectator and no longer a functioning warrior. Perhaps, too, I was a bit relieved.

Brum soon hobbled up to join us. I noticed blood on his fatigue pants.

"I got hit," he muttered in disgust and received aid from Bert for a bullet through his knee. I asked him about Pedro. Brum shook his head.

"Pedro didn't make it," he said.

We lay quietly for what seemed a long time. I looked over to Joe Briones. I reached out and stroked his black hair as a final goodbye. I was surprised to find it so thick and curly. I thought of his two kids and his wife, now a widow, in Rosemeade, California. She was Hispanic, and Joe, a Greek, spoke the Castilian dialect.

There was a young replacement soldier I didn't know from another platoon leaning against the only tree in the vicinity. He was supposed to be covering us, but he was shaking so violently he couldn't have hit a man at five yards. Someone sent him back, and, after a time, I was comforted to see Harris Choate arrive to take his place. Choate, a National Guardsman before Pearl Harbor, was one of the best marksmen in the division. He'd come in first with the M1 in his regiment during Basic Training. Of the ten men from my 2d platoon who'd come out to assist the 3d, Choate was the only one not killed or wounded.

My calm at watching events unfold was suddenly broken by a mortar shell exploding just a few yards uphill from us. The electric jolt to my hip hadn't zapped my fear of mortars. "Oh shit," I said, "that's all we need." But none of us was hit, and no more came.

After thirty minutes or so, a lull in the action permitted four scared green replacements from Headquarters Company to start evacuating us. Brumfield was the first to be loaded onto a makeshift litter, a poncho. Just as the soldiers grabbed the corners of the poncho, Brum let out a groan. A Japanese bullet had just ricocheted off the ground and blown two holes in his back.

"Goddamn you dirty cocksuckers, shooting a man when he's already hit!" shouted Brum.

I laughed a bit as the shaken replacements hurried Brum out of there.

Four new replacements came out for me. I introduced myself and extended my left hand in courtesy. They didn't respond, except with a funny look, and ignored the hand. They had no poncho, so they grabbed me under the arms and began to drag me. My lifeless right arm flopped about, getting in the way.

"Just take my hand and stick in the belt in the back," I suggested, trying to be helpful.

They did as I said but still had trouble lugging me without disturbing my wounds. Finally, we reached the top of a small hill, and they decided to slide me on my stomach down the other side.

"Hi-yo, Silver! Away!" I yelled as I pitched head-first forty yards down the wet grassy slope. This probably only confirmed to them my deranged state of mind.

I hit the bottom of the hill and landed in a large mud puddle. With my dead legs and my only good arm wedged under me, I found I could barely lift my face out of the brown water. The replacements, meanwhile, had forgotten me. They were standing a few feet away, talking excitedly about the day's action. I began to fear I'd survive my wounds only to drown in a mud puddle.

I raised my face to the side and lifted my mouth above the puddle like a freestyle swimmer getting a breath.

"Will somebody get me out of this water?" I croaked.

They guys jerked their heads up and came to my rescue. They put me on a litter and carried me to the battalion aid station. The doctor in charge, a major, gave me morphine and re-bandaged my wounds.

"You're lucky, Gruenfeld," he said, "it looks as though this is something that will get you back home without crippling you."

It was late in the afternoon, still raining, and getting dark already. A fierce Japanese artillery barrage shook the earth and rattled nerves. But we were safe from it here in defilade on the reverse side of a slope. The cots in my tent soon filled up with the newly wounded. About forty of us awaited further evacuation.

My fighting part of the war was over. All that remained was a long journey home.

CHAPTER TWO

Basic Training

࿇✿࿇

In war, a boy is often asked to play the man and, in the playing, he becomes one. I'd been practicing for the role of warrior since at least 1932, when at age eight, I received a single shot Winchester Model 04 .22 rifle from my dad. He wasn't a hunter and normally displayed the common sense characteristic of his solid German Midwestern engineer background. I have no idea what made him depart from it on this occasion. Perhaps somehow he saw my destiny and sought to prepare me for it. I spent the next decade putting hundreds of rounds through that rifle and, later, an old Winchester pump .22 in an attempt to de-populate the countryside of gophers, crows, blackbirds, and squirrels, when in season. It was training that would serve me well in the Pacific.

Here I am at age eight in 1933 at Gerhams Lake, Wisconsin, holding a Winchester .22 slide action with hammer. (*Author's collection*)

Two years before I received that gift, in 1930, my younger sister Barbara Jean died. She was four years old, a sweet innocent beauty who trailed me wherever I went. That spring, she developed a sore throat and low-grade fever. They didn't go away. Her lymph nodes swelled. Breathing and swallowing became difficult. Doctors diagnosed diphtheria, a bacterial infection virtually unknown in the United States today but a scourge in the 1920s when as many as 15,000 children died of it each year. A new vaccine had just been developed, but it still wasn't common to have children inoculated, and Barbara Jean never was. She died at home, just before Christmas.

My parents blamed themselves. My mother was especially despondent. She sat for days, weeks, staring wordlessly out the living room window of our solid orange brick duplex on North Sacramento Avenue on Chicago's North Side. The window faced south, and she'd watch through the wintry twilight until the sun arced below the two-story apartment buildings across the street. I wasn't tended to that much then, but I didn't care. I had an active imagination fed by magazines, books, and radio programs like "Tarzan of the Apes." All my daydreams dealt with adventures in the wilderness, places far away from our leafy Chicago neighborhood.

Some of these adventures came to life for me as an indirect result of Barbara Jean's death. In her grief, my mother moved us frequently to her parents' house in McHenry, a town of 1,200 on the Fox River named after an old Indian fighter. My father often commuted from his job in Chicago about fifty miles to the southeast. Tucked away near the Wisconsin border, McHenry was surrounded by lakes and streams, moraine hills and peat bogs. It was a rough boy's paradise, and I was given unusual leeway—too much perhaps—to spend entire days alone in the woods and along the streams. We spent every weekend, holiday, and summer in McHenry, and it was there that I did most of my learning and growing. I went to school and lived in Chicago, but I dreamed in McHenry. McHenry was home.

A home provides sanctuary, and I felt as safe and comfortable in the forests of McHenry as anywhere else. The trees especially welcomed me into their arms, very high up indeed for a five-year-old. I began practicing for the role of Tarzan's sidekick, in case the jungle hero should ever need one. I wasn't sure about the qualifications. Was 4'9" tall enough? What would a try-out for such a job entail? Tree-climbing had to be a big part of it, so I set my own challenges accordingly. My goal was always to clamber high enough into the leafy crown so that by hugging a limb I could sway with the tree in the breeze. My acrobatics grew more elaborate. By the time I was eight, my favorite tree-climbing spot was on a hillside by the Fox River. There I would scramble fifteen feet up in a chokecherry, reach out and barely catch hold of a neighboring hickory branch and swing a couple feet to where I could straddle a flexible water birch limb. I would ride it down until it caught in the forked top of another water birch where I would slide on the smooth trunk to the ground and then repeat the process.

The summer I was ten, I began taking day-long hikes, probably not getting over two miles from home, with only my dog Patch for company. The high adventure on these tramps through the hardwood lots around Lake Defiance often involved Patch being chased by cows. At first I cried, but then I saw just how quick and alert Patch was. My fear abated. I learned to trust in skill. But I wisely remained wary of bulls.

My father encouraged my outdoor activities. He was an avid fisherman and fashioned a pole for me out of a willow switch when I was four, and I caught fish with it. My grandfather Anton Johnson was another influence. He came from a land of trees and water, Norway. He'd immigrated to America in 1872, when his native Oslo was still known as "Christiania." He'd made a small fortune manufacturing men's waistcoats. For decades, these vests were an essential part of any man's wardrobe. His fortune declined drastically when fashions changed in the 1920s, but he retained his hardy Norwegian attitude. In 1937 at age eighty-six, he grabbed an axe and chopped down a red oak tree that was two-feet in diameter. The exertion pulled muscles around his heart. He died soon after.

My ventures into the woods with my grandfather

involved the fall harvest of hickory nuts. He'd crack them carefully in a vice and pry out the meat with a nut picker. He'd hand out one-pound candy boxes of hickory nut halves as Christmas presents. Smaller pieces went into pies, cakes, and bread, or were popped into our mouths. Trees, I learned, were things of beauty that provide people what they need.

I had a few friends who would accompany me on my explorations, but most of the time I was alone. Spending days by myself casting in a river or stream, hunting wildlife, or climbing trees never bothered me. On the contrary, my solitude in nature intensified the almost mystical feelings of comfort and awe I experienced in the woods. These feelings have never left me. In war, trees can be dangerous. They harbor snipers and can detonate mortar and artillery shells, causing deadly downward explosions. Yet, on Luzon, I always felt comfortable when surrounded by trees. In later years, when I ran across William Blake's observation that "A fool sees not the same tree a wise man sees," I knew just what he meant.

My fascination with all things out-of-doors no doubt distracted me from happenings elsewhere. I never noticed, for example, that my father was unemployed for two years during the Depression. He lost his job at an engineering firm in 1937, but continued his daily routine of leaving the house at 7:30 a.m. and returning at 5:30 p.m. Only long afterward did I discover that he spent this time inquiring about jobs and keeping up his contacts. Relatives helped us out financially, and my mother made a few dollars selling lingerie. I peddled magazines (*Colliers, Ladies Home Journal*, and *Saturday Evening Post*) door-to-door at age eight, before moving on to caddying and concessions at McHenry Country Club. We never had much money, but I lacked nothing important. In 1936, I spent a hard-earned $6.95 on a brand-new .410 single shot Eastern Arms shotgun at Sears Roebuck. I had everything I needed.

School happened for me. Despite my voracious appetite for books, I was a B- student. I could name all the trees of the forest and ace *Field and Stream's* multiple choice deer hunting tests (though I'd never been within 100 miles of a deer, which were absent from Illinois' forests in those days), but I had a tough time mustering up enthusiasm for academic subjects. With a November birthday, I was pretty young compared to my classmates and made younger when I skipped a grade after my family moved to another apartment and I entered new school. It seems there weren't enough of us in seventh grade, so the school placed us in eighth. This age disparity didn't bother me, but kept me a bit out of sync with the rest of my classmates.

Two activities absorbed my interest when at age twelve I entered Carl Schurz High School, a massive complex of brick buildings on North Milwaukee Avenue. The first was swimming. It suited my long strong arms and endurance, as well as my penchant for individual sports. I specialized in the backstroke and eventually became team captain.

My father encouraged a second activity: the Reserve Officers' Training Corps, or ROTC. ROTC for high school students was created in 1916, the year before the United States' entry into World War I. My father's service in what he called "The Great War" fascinated me, though he talked of it little. There were few stories, but one heroic image made a deep impression. My dad said that as a litter bearer, he and others would lie on top of the wounded when the shelling got bad. I pictured my old father sprawled atop a stretcher bearing a bloody American soldier while shells burst in the air like fireworks.

Dad had a relic of the war that filled in some of the gaps of his service record. I have it today. It's a brass matchbox cover made from a shell case, inscribed with details of his military career. He was drafted at age thirty-one in 1918 and shipped overseas less than two months later to the 53d

Pioneer Infantry. He was in France before he even fired a rifle. Saint-Mihiel, the battle that saw one of the first American uses of tanks and airplanes in combat, was his first action as a litter bearer. Next was the Meuse-Argonne Offensive, our bloodiest campaign of the war, 120,000 American casualties. Dad returned home in May of 1919 as a corporal after a short tour in the Ordnance Corps.

Dad thought that his twelve-year-old son would enjoy the ROTC, and he was right. We learned history, civics, military maneuvers and field problems, and were given ample time on the rifle range, where I excelled. We wore our uniforms to school on Fridays, a khaki shirt and tie under an Army serge jacket with brass buttons. When I graduated from Carl Schurz with 703 others in May of 1941, I was sixteen years old and had achieved the rank of Captain. Another step in my preparation.

****

On the afternoon of Sunday, December 7, 1941, I was aboard the Illinois Central train heading to Urbana-Champaign to complete my first semester at the University of Illinois. I'd just been home for a short visit. At a stop on the line, someone mentioned that Pearl Harbor had been attacked by the Japanese. I knew where Pearl Harbor was, and my ROTC classes had made me aware of the world situation. There was a big global war going on, and I'd assumed that the United States would be drawn into it and so would I. When I reached my Delta Chi fraternity house, a couple of students had already packed their bags and gone home to enlist, skipping finals. It was that kind of war.

I had just turned seventeen. "It will be a long war," I said to myself. "I have time." Besides, there were a few things I wanted to do before heading overseas.

One of them was to go out West. Despite so-so grades, I devoured my pre-Forestry studies at the university. That first semester gave me a quick overview of the role of forests and foresters throughout the world. Trees became an obsession. I wanted to learn to identify them all, especially the big ones out West, where I vowed to live if I survived the war. On campus, I'd go out of my way to walk past the stately white and Ponderosa pines near the Armory. Just looking at them and drinking in their aroma induced a state of pleasure that was almost sensual.

In the spring of 1942, I applied for a summer job with the United States Forest Service. With the war draining manpower and Franklin Roosevelt's Civilian Conservation Corps coming to an end, the Forest Service needed people to fight fires and battle blister rust, a disease that was devastating western white pine. In early June, I boarded a glistening streamliner, the Great Northern Railroad's Empire Builder, and headed West. We cut northwest through Wisconsin and Minnesota before paralleling North Dakota's and Montana's long borders with Canada. My eyes were glued to the window each day, all day, until the last bit of daylight was extinguished and the Great Plains disappeared into the blackness. By the time we reached Coeur d'Alene, Idaho, I'd seen deer, bear, antelope, prairie dogs, and a coyote. I was now, in my heart, a Westerner.

We trucked from Coeur d'Alene to Magee Ranger Station in the Idaho Panhandle National Forest. Our bunkhouse had wooden floors and knee walls with a canvas tent roof. We didn't fight enough fires for my liking and spent most of our days pulling plants of the genus Ribes, mostly currants and gooseberries, that served as alternate hosts for the blister rust. We spent much time falling "big snags," dead trees that we used for firewood. I was young and fit and newly adept at the crosscut saw. I swelled with pride when an old Idaho sawyer named One Armed John suggested I skip the next semester and join him falling white pine for the Ohio Match Company. "You and I can make good money," he said.

John taught me the art of getting logs to roll downhill and land right on the road where they could be bucked into firewood length. Using cant-hooks and Peaveys, John could aim the log to hit stumps and other obstructions en route to slow it down and change its direction and thus achieve perfect placement. Such hand-logging skill was impressive, considering some of the logs were three feet or more in diameter and weighed a couple of tons, while the hills had sixty-percent grades.

One day John couldn't be with us so he said, "Just fall and buck a couple of snags. Don't try to roll 'em."

My seventeen-year-old partner and I couldn't help ourselves. We felled a seventy-foot larch and bucked it into five or so logs. The butt log looked like it would roll easily to the road with a little help from us. We pooled our intelligence and carefully plotted the route. The large end, we figured, would hit a high stump, then a big log which would shift its direction toward another stump, from where it would be delivered to its proper place on the road.

The 3,000 pound butt log hit its marks but careened past the road at twenty-miles-per-hour and plunged into a canyon 600 feet below. The next day John asked no questions, and we didn't volunteer anything.

I was tempted by John's offer to work with him through the fall, but was also committed to college, the ROTC, and the war effort I knew I'd soon be joining.

Besides that, I had a girlfriend. I'd seen her at the university swimming pool at the end of my freshman year. I didn't get her name, so I looked through every photograph in the yearbook until I discovered her identity: Ruth Oksendahl. She was a year older than I was and came from a solid Norwegian family. I'd been rather shy with girls, and this was my first serious relationship. We were going pretty steady when I turned eighteen in November.

Ruth probably delayed my entry into the service. I enjoyed dating her and wasn't keen on leaving. As an ROTC cadet, I was on track to go to Officer Candidate School or enter the Army Specialized Training Program at the end of my sophomore year. Either way, I'd join the Army as an officer in the spring of 1943 after further training. Ruth and I had until then, at least.

As that date approached, I grew impatient to get in on the action. I gave my future more serious thought. I was in top physical condition, knew I was a good shot, and wanted to test myself against the best the military and the enemy had to offer. The Air Corps was the most glamorous branch of service, but I had no interest in fighting the war at 25,000 feet. The Marines I thought too aggressive. I wanted to use my head. Being acquainted with the Forest Service's nascent smoke-jumper program, where firefighters parachuted into wildfire zones, I aspired to become a paratrooper. I knew the training was rigorous and the missions dangerous, and that's why I considered the Airborne the most elite of fighting forces.

With my mind set on the Airborne, I now had no use for OCS. I didn't want to enter paratrooper training as an eighteen-year-old officer. That seemed like skipping ahead to me. I didn't need the ROTC anymore, nor college classes. My mind was made up and waiting on the inevitable became intolerable to me. So, in April 1943, with only a couple weeks to go until the completion of my second semester of sophomore year, I quit school and said goodbye to Ruth. She had two brothers in the service, one in the Marines, one in the Air Corps. Both would die, one on Iwo Jima. She understood my eagerness to get overseas.

By this time, my parents also understood. Shortly before induction, my father, the old Pioneer Infantryman and stretcher bearer, sat me down for a talk. He was man of few words, not due to any reticence on his part but rather to a remarkable economy of verbiage. Dad had the keen mind of an engineer and the ability to put things succinctly, though he had only a two-year associate engineering degree.

"I want to talk with you about C & C, Caution and Cunning," he said. "In dangerous situations, you must keep thinking. Always be thinking." He pointed to his head for emphasis. "Be cunning like a fox. Keep alert so you can think your way out of a problem. That's what courage is: the ability to keep your head when in danger. You're physically strong, but toughness is mental. Keep thinking through your exhaustion. Always keep thinking, and be cautious."

I was better at the thinking part.

****

I was inducted into the Army on April 15, 1943 at Fort Sheridan just north of Chicago. Five days later, I boarded a coach train at Union Station to take me to Camp Croft Infantry Replacement Training Center near Spartanburg, South Carolina, for fourteen weeks of Basic Training. Camp Croft was just then building a reputation for turning out what General George Patton called "class A fighting men," and I was ready for it. Before we pulled out, a matronly woman representing some civic club inspected our car for cleanliness. She wiped the windowsills with a white handkerchief,

Posing with my parents on April 15, 1943, the day I was inducted into the Army at Fort Sheridan. (*Author's collection*)

turned it over and nodded approvingly. We made our way through eastern hardwood forests tinged with the delicate pink of blooming dogwoods. We slept sitting up.

Unlike many recruits, I thrived in Basic Training. My first day, a trainee with some prior experience handed me a thing of beauty crafted from walnut, leather, and machined steel. The .30 caliber M1 Garand semi-automatic rifle weighed just short of ten pounds and felt like a stubby club. The trainee taught us how to field strip and reassemble the M1, and I was issued one of my own, serial number 639011.

I was assigned to 3d platoon, D Company, 39th Battalion, which had a bloated complement of fifty-two men ranging in age from eighteen-year-old kids like me to an old-timer, Wenzlick, who was thirty-five. We were a cross-section of white America. Half were northern, half southern. Some were grade school drop-outs, others college graduates. We came from big cities, small towns, and farms, mostly from east of the Mississippi. My squad of fourteen had a typical mix of American names. In addition to Wenzlick and me there was Schindler, Hall, Bruce, Barnwell, Davis, Nelson, Black, Sczymakowski, Kudranowicz, Sandelski, Dellicarpini, and Mirandola.

The training was rigorous and prepared us well for combat. Bayonet and hand-to-hand fighting, long hikes with full field packs, map and compass reading, weapons training, and the obstacle course built our confidence and made us feel like soldiers. Our week on the rifle range was especially fine. Before we even stepped foot on the range, we had to put in two full weeks of intensive non-firing marksmanship training. I wrote to my parents and complained about the finger blister I got: "Yesterday, we spent four hours doing nothing but dry firing by squeezing the trigger, or pushing back the bolt handle so your partner could squeeze the trigger.... Next week, we get up at 4:30 and with full field 'equip' walk three miles to the range [for live firing]. At 11:00 we come in three miles for lunch. Out three miles after lunch and back three miles for late supper. That is going to be very hot and pretty tough."

It *was* tough. But hearing quail calls and smelling the honeysuckle as we marched through shady draws lessened my fatigue. And the long hikes were worth it because we spent all day at the range among stacked M1s and piles of empty brass cartridges. We talked of nothing but shooting. I was in my element.

We practiced a lot, and then we fired for record. The lowest qualifying grade was Marksman, then Sharpshooter. To achieve Expert, the highest grade, one had to score 185. There was no guarantee a good shot would make a good soldier, nor was it easy to predict who would excel on the rifle range. One recruit in our company had never fired a weapon before and scored an Expert. Audie Murphy, by contrast, had grown up in rural Texas

Also taken on April 15, 1943, this photo shows me with my cousin, J. Oliver Buslee, who would serve as a B-17 pilot in Europe with the Eighth Air Force, 384th Bomb Group, 545th Squadron. J. Oliver would go down with his plane over Magdeburg, Germany, on September 28, 1944. (*Author's collection*)

shooting game for his family. Yet this most highly decorated soldier with 241 confirmed kills in Europe only qualified as a Marksman with the M1. I suspect the recoil of the ten-pound Garand was initially too much for the diminutive Murphy. He preferred the lighter carbine, which doesn't buck back so fiercely, and machine guns.

I was determined to qualify as an Expert in the M1 Garand. After all, I'd spent thousands of hours hunting in the woods around Lake Defiance. My eyes were superb, 20/15 in each without glasses, despite astigmatism. And they usually didn't blink when I fired.

We shot the M1 in three positions—standing, kneeling, prone—at ranges of 200, 300, and prone only at 500 yards. At 200 and 300 yards, it was either slow fire, one shot at a time, or rapid fire, one shot followed by a new clip and eight quick rounds. I mastered it all quickly, and in my final practice round I took nineteen shots, almost all bulls eyes, and scored the highest in the battalion. When I fired for record, however, I felt the pressure. My score dropped seven points. I still made Expert, barely.

We then moved to the Browning Automatic Rifle, or BAR, a different weapon altogether. A kind of hybrid of an M1 Garand and light machine gun, the BAR weighed fifteen pounds plus a twenty round magazine and had a selection lever for switching between single shot or automatic fire. The highest possible score with a BAR was 125, with 106 qualifying for Expert. All firing was at 200 yards. There were twenty-five shots in three arrangements: fifteen standing for rapid fire (thirty-five seconds); five shots prone and five shots kneeling for slow fire. The secret to getting a good score was not to fire over two shots in a burst. I was lucky enough to get a weapon with a sensitive trigger. I shot a 115 and won my second Expert Badge.

The light machine gun was the third and final weapon I fired for record. I was a little concerned because the sight radius—the distance between the front and rear sights—was so short that the front sight would blur despite my excellent vision. There was also a big variation in the quality of the guns. Again, I got lucky and drew a fine weapon for the record firing, which was done at 1,000 inches (83 feet or 27.8 yards). To hit a target at 1,000 inches, I set my sights at 400 yards. Bullets travel in an arc and, therefore, cross the line of sight twice, once going up and again coming down. We fired a total of ninety-six rounds in strings of forty-eight. We were urged to shoot in bursts of three at fifteen two-inch squares arranged in three groups of five, one vertical, one horizontal, and one diagonal. To score high, we had to hit each of the fifteen squares. I tried hard to squeeze off single shots in order to be as accurate as possible. It wasn't easy since the sensitive trigger fired six or seven rounds per second.

After firing, I wrote home. "I held that leaping gun down with a grip of iron," I bragged, "and fired 220 out of 256 for another Expert bar. I kind of like the old LMG [light machine gun] now."

Our week on the range was intended not only to get us used to firing but receiving fire. Instructors taught us what airborne bullets sounded like from various angles and distances. We spent time under the targets in protected bunkers called butts. The bullets whizzed by a couple feet from our heads. During slow firing, our job was to pull down the targets after each round and mark the hole (if any) for the shooter. M1 bullets traveled at three times the speed of sound, so they arrived before we ever heard the firing. I quickly learned the distinctive sound sequence of rifle fire: a crack overhead followed by the pop of the rifle going off. Crack…pop. Crack…pop. Over time, I learned how to estimate distance by timing the intervals between the sounds. By listening for the pop, one could also determine the direction of the shooter. This ability to judge the location of fire by sound proved an important combat skill.

There was something exhilarating about such exposure to danger. We were put in harm's way but also taught the skills necessary to stay safe. I learned it was possible to keep my head when under fire and outwit the enemy—such knowledge was a comfort…and a thrill.

We'd all heard about the Infiltration Course at Camp Croft—our Baptism by Fire—as soon as we'd arrived. It was a 100-yard crawl with rifle and full field pack through mud and barbed wire with live machine guns and nitrostarch charges going off. Many feared it. Stories circulated about the guy who came face-to-face with a snake on the course, reflexively started to his knees, and was cut apart by the machine gun. I couldn't wait.

The training cadre first ordered us to lie down on our backs with our heads against an earthen mound and our faces to the sky. Machine guns fired tracer bullets not two feet above our faces. The bullets struck the mound next to our heads with force. My stomach churned a little. Then, with our rifles in hand, we flipped over and pulled ourselves forward, wriggling and squirming like earthworms as we tried to stay as low as possible. Loud eruptions of nitrostarch bracketed our advance and splashed mud in our faces. Everyone in our platoon made it through, but some others froze terror-stricken. They simply couldn't move.

The machine guns had to be stopped for cadre to come in and pull the paralyzed out. For me, again, the experience was exhilarating, as close to combat as I would get for now.

My only complaint about Camp Croft pertained to hand grenade training. There wasn't enough of it. The Army was so short of grenades they allowed us only one live throw in all of Basic Training. In my case, the target was a mock-up mortar position. Most of our instruction seemed intended to scare us about the dangers of these twenty-ounce Mark 2 "pineapples." The trainers treated them like big artillery rounds. Consequently, we threw them way too soon after pulling the pin instead of allowing a second or two to tick off the 4.6-second fuses so the enemy wouldn't have time to throw them back. I wouldn't make that mistake overseas.

Although we couldn't train with live grenades, we could throw as many empty ones as we wanted. I took to spending my free time—evening hours after chow and Sundays—giving myself extra training. Another recruit, a Westerner and middleweight boxer named Tom Galt, shared my enthusiasm for this Army life. He and I became fast friends and together we threw hundreds of dummy grenades from every conceivable distance and angle at the mock pillboxes and building facades set up on our training grounds. We were like two kids, pockets full of rocks, knocking bottles off fence posts. But the throwing was serious. We compared our hang times to see if we'd be able to get our grenades to explode in the air. I discarded the official Army method of throwing—a kind of stiff-armed roundhouse—in favor of a baseball hurl. By keeping my bicep tight, I could get the height and distance I needed without injuring my arm.

Tom and I ran the obstacle course on our own for fun, clambering up and down walls, swinging monkey-like on a rope across a water pit, and otherwise crawling, hopping, and jumping our way through the 150-yard course. We tried to outdo each other on the twenty-foot high cargo nets by gripping the verticles and lowering ourselves down with our arms alone, feet dangling below. Basic Training put me in fighting shape and made me an absolute model soldier.

In fact, I worried I was a little too good. As an eighteen-year-old non-drinking, non-smoking virgin who had never been in a barfight, and hardly even a bar, I imagined real combat soldiers as rougher, worldlier, and more swaggering than I. Some of my Camp Croft cohort were as eager for combat as I, but not many. An equal number were just as eager to avoid frontline duty. The rest were in between. I didn't like the idea of coming across as a first sergeant's pet, a smooth-faced recruit without the nerve or initiative to break the rules. So, I decided to cause some trouble. One night, I started a world-class pillow fight.

Basic Training was nearing its end, and we were lounging in our second-floor barracks. I picked up a pillow and whacked another guy with it. The surprised soldier flung his own down-stuffed sack in return. Others joined in, taking one side or another or no side at all, swinging pillows with reckless abandon until the entire barracks had erupted in the largest pillow fight in the history of Basic Training. A couple of pillows broke, and tiny feathers filled the room, adding to the mayhem. The corporal in charge of the barracks walked in and nabbed me as a ringleader, along with a few other guys. He swore he'd bring us up on charges for courts-martial. Nothing ever came of it. I succeeded in muddying my reputation just enough, but not too much.

Our fourteen weeks of Basic Training climaxed in ten days of maneuvers, field exercises to get us ready for life in a war zone. We headed out early morning with sixty-pound field packs toward a predetermined point. Our platoon leader got lost, and we ended up walking twenty-nine miles that first day instead of twenty-five. Field problems came in rapid succession, day and night, in the heat and rain, testing all we'd learned during our training. We slept in shelter halves and battled chiggers…and crab lice from our temporary latrines. The latter bothered me especially. I found the infestation mentally disturbing, more so than any combat-related peril. With three days to go, the common cold I'd been nursing spiked into a 103.5 degree fever. I had to be evacuated from the field by ambulance. In the hospital, I received the diagnosis: nasopharyngitis.

I recovered quickly, but the Army wouldn't graduate me from Basic Training. My cohort left Camp Croft. I stayed behind. They received their overseas assignments, all Europe, while I waited to re-take my maneuvers with another training battalion. During this lull, I was assigned to one of the few disagreeable noncoms I'd encountered since joining the Army. First Sergeant Wrickson was a first-class son-of-a-bitch who didn't like me perhaps because I was an ROTC "college boy."

Wrickson merely amplified my growing impatience with training camp and my resolve to get on with the war. I'd gotten to the point where I was trained out. I couldn't imagine putting off my rendezvous with destiny any longer. I wanted to get into combat as soon as I could. I still admired the paratroopers, but the thought of enduring another eight weeks of training was intolerable. I determined to stay in the regular infantry. What the dogfaces lacked in prestige they more than made up for in action, and action is what I wanted.

For a while, it looked like the Army wouldn't cooperate with my plan. There was a need for MPs in August 1943, and I was told I was heading to a Military Police Battalion. I kicked and pleaded with every officer who'd listen until those orders were changed. Then, I found out they wanted to keep me as training cadre. Again, I protested. "I want to go into combat!" I demanded. The Army, accustomed to men who wanted out of the infantry rather than into it, finally relented and issued orders for me to report to Fort Meade after ten days leave.

I was going home and had one foot aboard a westbound train at the Spartanburg Union Station on Magnolia Street when a man behind me put his hand on my shoulder.

"Is your name Gruenfeld?" the man asked. "There's been a mistake in your orders. You can't leave."

I knew about the mistake. My two years in advanced ROTC at the University of Illinois entitled me to a rank of sergeant, three stripes. I'd gone through Basic Training as a private. I was paid as a private and treated like a private. That was fine with me. It's not that I didn't want the stripes. I just felt I hadn't earned them yet.

I traveled to Fort Meade after home leave. I endured another week of training and received the M1 Garand I would use throughout my time in the Pacific: serial number 1051653. Its parts were stamped, not machined, but the rifle functioned beautifully.

One cold gray day, after a long march, the training cadre sat us down and prepared us for an artillery bombardment. They wanted to give us a sense of the noise and concussion. About 200 yards away, they said, a dozen 105mm shells fired from howitzers would go off just above the ground all at once. It was called Time-on-Target, delivering a maximum of destructive force. The guns fired. Seconds later came a shock wave powerful enough to shake us. CAAR-UUM! It scared us a lot. The cadre advised us to get used to it because our side would be employing it a lot in combat. They never told us the enemy had it too.

I used a weekend pass to see Baltimore and gain a bit more of the experience I imagined a combat soldier should have. I entered a tavern and ordered my first drink: a Stinger, which was brandy and crème de menthe. The mint disguised the taste of the alcohol, and the drink went down easy. I walked a street lined with those trademarked Baltimore rowhouses with stoops right on the sidewalk. A door creaked open, revealing a Gypsy lady with a colorful scarf and earrings. She looked at me and curled her index finger in an inviting gesture.

I'd been told of the dangers of fortune tellers and other streetwise characters and watched my back as I stepped into her house and sat down at the crystal ball. I paid my three dollars up front. She opened my palms and studied them, then consulted the ball. She told me I'd be heading overseas.

"Don't worry," she assured me. "You'll make it home alive."

I'm sure she said that to all the boys with three dollars to blow.

CHAPTER THREE

Journey into War

December 1943—July 1944

By early December 1943, my possessions had been boiled down to what I could carry in my field pack and Army duffel. Almost all of it was Army issue, with the exceptions of pencils and paper, a Bible, and a cheap book of Rudyard Kipling poems.

Drizzle fell from a gray sky over Camp Shanks, "Last Stop, U.S.A.," the largest port of embarkation in the United States. The sleepy farm village of Orangeburg, New York, had ballooned to a city of 50,000 in three months. Empty fields were replaced by Quonset huts, chapels, stores, a theater, a laundry, a bakery, a hospital, and row upon row of wooden 20' x 100' barracks, each heated by three pot-bellied stoves.

I shared one of those barracks with forty-nine other men for about a week. We did little but wait. A final field inspection confirmed that we were fully equipped and our gear was in good condition. We were put on alert, told we'd be shipping out within twelve hours, and then marched to a train station for a short ride to the ferry terminal at Weehawken, New Jersey. We crossed the Hudson River to the finger piers on Manhattan's West Side. Gray clad ships lined perpendicular to the shore awaited our boarding. MPs kept watch. If anyone was going to go AWOL, this would be the time.

My ship, the S.S. *Santa Cruz*, made a none-too-formidable first impression. The old Grace Line steamer was of pre-World War I vintage and had spent the past thirty years hauling timber from South America. Now, it was outfitted to carry 800 men to a war zone. We descended into dark holds studded with pipe frameworks. On those frames were canvas shelves reaching to the ceiling. These were our bunks. The tightly stretched rectangles measured two-feet wide by six-feet long with only eighteen inches clearance between the layers. Within hours, it seemed, the hold filled up with the odors of many men. Once we hit the seas, more odors would follow. But I was happy. For, unlike the neighboring ships on the West Side pier, ours was heading to the Pacific.

Until we boarded, I'd assumed we were bound for Europe, the destination of most soldiers. I was a bit unusual in wanting to fight the Japanese. Revenge for Pearl Harbor played a small part in my preference. I wanted to see the jungle. The prospect of large-scale combat in European cities didn't intrigue me nearly as much as that of hunting the enemy in the wilderness. I imagined exciting combat on exotic islands with big trees, vibrant flora, and wild animals. My imaginings weren't too far off.

One downside to this stroke of good luck was that the *Santa Cruz* didn't seem to be in any hurry to get us to our destination. We chugged out of the harbor on December 6, 1943 without a convoy and made our way south toward the Caribbean. For the next forty-five days, we'd be at sea.

U-boats still patrolled the Atlantic coast, but the emergency drills we practiced lacked a sense of urgency. Our Captain possessed great faith in the *Santa Cruz's* watertight bulkheads. "It will take much more than one torpedo to sink us," he announced.

We passed the time reading, gambling, and trading our short life stories. I befriended another Chicagoan, Bob Dvorak, who, like me, was eager to test his mettle in combat. I finished ten books

on the *Santa Cruz*; *Lust for Life* by Irving Stone
and *Life in a Putty Knife Factory* by H. Allen Smith
were the best. I lost some money playing poker
and craps. All of us spent hours shuffling in the
two daily chow lines that wound up and down
stairs, through various holds and bulkheads, and
around the deck before ending in the galley. The
queue killed time, but the food that awaited at
the end of it seemed intended to kill us. The coffee
was even worse. I'd been issued an aluminum cup,
which nested in my canteen. The cup was cor-
roded, and hard as I tried, I couldn't scrub it clean.
After a few days holding what the cooks on the
Santa Cruz called coffee, the cup shined like new.

Despite the discomforts, I grew to like the sea
and understood the fascination many men have
with it. I escaped the hold with my woolen blanket,
which I used on deck as a mattress at night. The
sunsets were unfailingly magnificent, and I spent
hour after hour on the ship's bow watching sea
snakes, flying fish, and dolphins in the Caribbean.

Soon after leaving the Panama Canal, we ran
into boiler trouble, and our already torpid pace
crawled almost to a stop. As we drifted on the
slow bell, an enormous Hawksbill turtle glided
leisurely past us. We roared with laughter and
wondered aloud whether the war would end before
we got into it.

One morning, a shout broke our monotony. "There's a mine!"

Less than a hundred yards away floated a three-foot diameter metal sphere studded with horns and festooned with seaweed. If anything hit the horns, the mine would explode. We thought it a good idea to detonate the mine with rifle fire, but our Captain, rumor had it, ordered it to be left alone. He was afraid an explosion would alert enemy submarines to our presence. I disapproved the decision, as did many other soldiers, and imagined with rue another troop ship running into the mine at night.

Our arrival in New Caledonia proved even more exciting than anticipated when a typhoon struck the island shortly after we anchored. We stayed aboard as the winds gusted to eighty miles per hour and the old ship's metal-plated hull screamed and groaned. Sailors on shore gripped each other conga-line style as they struggled to lash our ship to the dock. Further back, behind the sailors, the wind was tearing apart a lumberyard. Lumber blew about like leaves.

Our tent camp was destroyed, so we remained on the ship for a while until it could be rebuilt. Then, we marched to our pyramidal tents and stacked our barracks bags around the center pole. Soon, I saw my first casualty of war. A soldier was

cleaning his rifle which had a shell in the chamber.
The rifle fired, and the round hit another soldier
in the head several tents away. Medics toted the
lifeless body on a litter. I'd witness many more accidental firings before the war was over.

We quickly redeployed to a Replacement Training Center near Noumea, the principle city on
this French colonial island. We trained little, and
had only the lightest of duties. The streets of
Noumea were strangely barren of women, French
or Melanesian. Every once in a while, a pair of
curious eyes would peak out from behind drapes,
but otherwise the young ladies were kept safely
out of American soldiers' reach.

I took advantage of our lull in activity to explore
the tropical dry forest surrounding our base. The
long narrow main island was actually the mountainous peak of a submerged continent, Zealandia,
that broke off from Australia tens of millions of
years ago, carrying diverse and unique life forms
with it. The Japanese had maneuvered on New
Caledonia before the war and had planned to in-
vade in 1942 before changing their minds. I saw
remnants of the Japanese military occupation in
the mountains, which were pocked with spooky
caverns.

For all my outdoor adventurousness, I've never
liked caves, and my exploration of them on New

Caledonia only confirmed my bias. One night, three soldiers and I took flashlights and, after a rocky mile's climb, entered an eerie opening in the mountain. We were about forty yards in when we came to a place where the roof had caved in leaving a small dark hole. I shined my light into the blackness with the other men on either side of me. There was a loud screech and a huge black bat flew directly at us. We all fell backward, and I dropped the light. I scuttled about on my hands and knees in the darkness until I found it. When I clicked it on, I saw I was alone. That ended my cave explorations.

The beaches and lagoons of New Caledonia were more to my liking. This was my first time on a saltwater beach, and I was mesmerized by the aquamarine ocean teeming with fish, all brilliantly colored, and a few sharks. I rented a dugout canoe from a native and trolled off shore, only to be swamped by two-foot high waves. I also body-surfed when the waves were bigger and took long hikes down along the estuaries. Brightly colored crabs littered the mud banks but scrambled into their holes at my slightest approach. I tried sneaking up on them, but no matter how quietly I tip-toed, they darted out of sight. I even experimented to see if they would scatter when I blinked my eyes. They didn't.

These tropical adventures distracted me for a while from my impatience for action. Bob Dvorak and I made our eagerness for combat clear to a sympathetic colonel and asked him to transfer us to the Americal Division. This storied division had been hurriedly created and deployed to protect New Caledonia after Pearl Harbor ("Americal" was short for "American, New Caledonian"). Part of the division had fought on Guadalcanal, and I wanted to join it on Bougainville, where it had recently relieved the 3d Marine Division. Our request went nowhere. The Army had other plans for us: more training in New Zealand.

After a rough passage with lots of seasickness, we arrived in New Zealand, and I was quickly enchanted by the dramatic and varied landscape, exotic fauna, and charming people. Kipling had been similarly smitten, and he captured my feeling for the land in the Auckland section of his poem, *The Song of the Cities:*

> Last, loneliest, loveliest, exquisite, apart—
> On us, on us the unswerving season smiles,
> Who wonder mid our fern why men depart
> To seek the Happy Isles.

Another Replacement Training Center awaited us. This time, however, we received an assignment.

We were made part of the 43d Infantry Division. I became a member of L Company, 103d Infantry Regiment, one of three regiments that made up the 43d.

The division I joined had first seen combat at the tail end of the Guadalcanal campaign, and played a key role in capturing the Munda airstrip on New Georgia Island. Casualties and illness had cut the division's fighting strength in half. We were there to replace those losses, and we largely kept our distance from the veterans at first. Initially, while we drilled and conditioned our bodies, the veterans took advantage of liberal pass privileges to enjoy Auckland and even travel to the South Island. Eventually, I led the 200 men of L Company daily in our physical training exercises. I prided myself in holding my M1 rifle out in front of me parallel to the ground longer than anyone else in the company wanted to.

A public relations sergeant assembled us in a big barn-like building on our base near Warkworth to teach us the history of our 103d Regiment, which had been part of the Maine National Guard. The sergeant regaled us with stories of heroism in the Civil War and World War I before delivering the regimental motto: "To the Last Man." That registered positively and was followed by a thoughtful silence. It ended when a loud voice

in the back of the room yelled, "Yeah, the Colonel."
The barn exploded with laughter, thus terminating
our orientation. I would sometimes think of this
incident when I saw our new regimental commander, Colonel Joe Cleland. Seldom, in fact, was
he the last man.

One of the first veterans I got to know in L
Company was Harry Nash, a grizzled machine
gun sergeant who had fought on New Georgia.
I'd just received my first weekend pass and was
waiting near camp with some other guys for a bus
to Auckland. Harry approached me. He wasn't
big but wiry and strong with a heavy bunch of
muscle high in his back, evidence of his past as a
pulpwood logger in Maine. Harry opened his wallet and pulled out a couple big bills.

"Gruenfeld, I know you men haven't been paid
for a long time and must be about broke. Take
this and pay me back when you can."

I demurred. But Harry insisted.

"You'll be doing me a favor," he explained. "I'll
just spend it if I keep it, and I have more."

I accepted with many thanks and had the warm
feeling you get when someone does you a favor in
exactly the right way.

A few weeks later at a weekend dance at a
Grange Hall, he and another noncom argued over
whom should dance with a certain lady and de-

cided to settle the matter with a fistfight. Harry looked to be outmatched by an opponent who was the regimental light heavyweight boxing champ and weighed at least twenty pounds more. Bystanders finally did have to stop the fight. Harry had knocked the champ down three times and might have really hurt him if they had let it continue.

Veterans like Harry usually didn't express any eagerness to get back into combat. The only one I met who did was a squad leader named Moody. Moody was a killer who used a sniper rifle. I asked him what combat was like.

"You know, it's pretty exciting stuff," he said.

An excellent soldier in the field, Moody couldn't stay out of trouble when he wasn't on the front lines. When I met him, he was a staff sergeant. A few months later in New Guinea, he was busted to private for brawling with some MPs. Once in combat on Luzon, he was back to sergeant, leading a squad through the roughest of fights.

Most of the new guys weren't gung-ho for battle either. A few actively sought a way out. One draftee laced his cigarettes with iodine and hoped that doctors would find spots on his lungs and disqualify him for duty. My own platoon leader in New Zealand, Lieutenant Smith, hated the Army and the war. I had dinner with him in Auckland one night with a New Zealand sergeant who'd just come back from fighting in North Africa and the Middle East. Smith grumbled to the sergeant that the United States shouldn't have entered the war even after Pearl Harbor. I made damn sure to tell this New Zealand patriot afterward that my lieutenant's opinion wasn't shared by the rest of us. Later, Smith deliberately held his hand on a rifle grenade perched at the end of an M1 barrel as another guy shot it. He wanted to tear up his hand so he'd be put out of action. He tore up his hand all right, but not enough to keep him out. Eventually, he was transferred to another platoon and killed by a machine gun on Luzon. I recall his last words: "There's no one up here."

I took measure of some of the other new guys like me. A few seemed born to lead men in battle, while others gave the impression that the Army had made a mistake accepting them for service. Squad leader Sergeant Tom DeLord had a tough demeanor, the physique of a body builder, and a face that looked chiseled from granite. Pfc. Leonard Posey, by contrast, possessed features I could only describe as girlish, even pretty. Likewise, one could easily imagine quiet and thin Pfc. Edwin Cooke in a choirboy's robes, and his non-drinking, non-smoking, non-swearing, and church-going habits reinforced the image. Only the three expert weapons badges on his blouse gave warning not to judge this boy on looks alone.

A few replacements shared my impatience for the battlefield. One of them was nineteen-year-old Louis Magrames from Mishiwaka, Indiana. A hulking six-foot-one and 220 pounds, Magrames didn't play down his rough-and-ready attitude.

"I want to kill some Japs," he'd say.

I sometimes asked him why he was so eager to fight the Japanese. The laconic Magrames would only reply, "I've got a grudge."

Chalmus Brammer, a tall lanky nineteen-year-old Texan, was probably typical of most replacements. He didn't express any burning interest in testing himself in combat, but he didn't show fear of it either. Bram was baby-faced and happy-go-lucky. He loved to joke around. He was, after all, like most of us, just a kid.

Soon after joining the 43d Division, I was given a squad of fourteen men to lead through training and then into battle. Most of these were replacements, but three were veterans with experience on New Georgia. One, a buck sergeant named Ashey, grumbled about being passed over for someone as green as I. With Ashey breathing down my neck, I made sure always to be far out front of my men in training, calisthenics, and every other activity. For good measure, I lied about my age. Everyone, from Colonel Cleland on down, assumed I was twenty-one, two years older than I really was.

After being in L Company about three months the company commander had a squad drill competition. This consisted of about ten minutes of close order drill by each of the approximately twelve squads in the company. My squad looked pretty good, kept in step, and I also gave them some fancy irregular commands. For example, while they were at attention with rifles on their shoulders I shouted, "Special order, ARMS!" Then, instead of doing it all together they did it one at a time. We won the competition. The prize was two cases of beer. Since I didn't drink, the men got it all.

Despite drilling to peak performance, I was plagued by a nagging source of self-doubt: the fact that I wasn't the ballroom brawler type I imagined most good combat soldiers to be. I wanted to prove my toughness, and a bully in another company gave me a chance to do so. One of the men in my squad, a tough seventeen-year-old named Jack Fraley, got into a chow-line argument with a big amateur boxer from Minnesota, Bergstrom. Preparing to fight, Fraley turned to hand his mess gear to the man behind and got blindsided by Bergstrom who knocked Fraley out cold and cut his lip so badly you could see teeth when his lips were supposed to be closed. L Company was enraged, but we had no plans for retaliation.

Then, my company commander approached me. "Gruenfeld," he said, "if you should happen to beat Bergstrom up, nothing will happen to you."

I took up the assignment with some trepidation, not for my physical safety but for my ability to do Bergstrom some damage before he could knock me out. I'd had some boxing and wrestling at the University of Illinois but had gotten clobbered some in a fight with the captain of my high school football team. A friend at the time had quipped that, as swim captain, I should have fought him in the deep end of a swimming pool.

I found Bergstrom in the mess hall on a Saturday and told him I was going to give him a chance to be a man and fight face-to-face.

"Meet me at the backroad crossing on Monday at 1600 hours," I said.

All weekend I worked on a fight plan that would allow me to hurt him before he put me out. By Monday afternoon, I was ready. I waited at the crossroad, but Bergstrom didn't show, so I went looking for him. He was in the mess hall again. I confronted him in a loud voice so others could hear.

"You're a yellow cocksucker!" I yelled. Then, I turned away.

That settled the matter, and Fraley appreciated my effort.

Our training ratcheted up in intensity as the spring of 1944 wore on, and I threw myself into it with new vigor. We operated on a strict schedule with small unit drills that lasted from reveille until 1600. The instructors would run us through a course where we fired as we pushed ahead and then hit the ground when satchel charges, designed to simulate artillery, exploded around us. Shots came from the rear as well, and friendly fire accidents became increasingly common.

We got weekends off, and we all spent much time in Warkworth or at the USO hall mixing with locals and enjoying the live orchestras the division provided. At one event, I danced with a pretty girl with a page boy haircut. A drunk soldier began harassing her to dance with him. I held him off with a threat. The girl's mother approached me afterward, thanked me for my chivalry, and invited me to her house for dinner. Thus began my brief and quite innocent love affair with the seventeen-year-old secretarial student Elra Brakenrig.

Elra and I went on dates to movies, dances, and church. We hardly touched each other, and my fourteen-man squad ribbed me to no end about it. In truth, I loved Elra's parents as much as I did

Photo of my New Zealand girlfriend,
Elra Brakenrig, age seventeen, in 1944.
(*Author's collection*)

her and became such a regular at their house that
they gave me my own bedroom. I would jog the
six or seven miles from our base camp to deliver
butter, rations, and other foodstuff they needed

and then would spend the day reading in the family's library or listening to records on their hand-cranked Victrola. I must have finished a half-dozen books on the Crusades in their house. Mrs. Brakenrig would cook up a wonderful dinner, and then the ladies would go off to bed, leaving Elra's father and me alone in the quiet darkened parlor. Mr. Brakenrig was County Clerk and had been a machine gunner in World War I. He'd fought with the ANZACS (Australian and New Zealand Army Corps) at the Battle of Gallipoli. He knew I was eager to get into combat and gently tried to rein in my enthusiasm for it. He didn't succeed.

I once learned a valuable combat lesson at the Brakenrig homestead. I often shot rabbits for the family for food. One day I brought an M1 carbine with me for that purpose. I hadn't trained much with a carbine, either in Basic Training or New Zealand, and wanted to see how this light-weight weapon handled. I spied a rabbit and pulled the trigger, hitting the animal in the stomach. The rabbit dragged himself toward the brush, and I shot it again in the same place. The rabbit still didn't die, and I knocked it in the head with my rifle butt. I told myself that if a carbine couldn't kill a rabbit with two shots, it likely wouldn't do a good job on the Japanese. I never used one again.

In mid-May, I kissed Elra for the first time. She

allowed it because our whole division was being loaded on to trucks for month-long maneuvers almost 200 miles south in the forests near Rotorua. The weather there was bitter cold, but the terrain almost magical. Bubbling mud pools, thermal springs, and towering redwoods and Radiata pines surrounded our bivouac near the base of a volcano and shore of a shallow lake. For the first time, live artillery was brought to bear on our training. We'd be given orders to attack a small hill. Our mortar squad would fire several rounds and then a squad or platoon would approach. Cut-out silhouettes of enemy soldiers would appear, and we'd have to react quickly and fire. All this on short sleep, cold rations, and long days of rough outdoor conditions.

Some say you can never adequately simulate the combat experience for training purposes. While it's true that there's an irreproducible quality to real live action, the training we received was essential to our success. I shudder to think what might have happened to us without it. I returned to Wackworth in mid-June fairly confident that I would hold up ok under fire.

On July 4, we were ordered on a fifteen mile hike. It being a holiday, we bitched and moaned about it more than usual. Nearing the end of the hike in Warkworth, our company commander surprised us with a two-hour beer break. The men made off immediately for the hardware store where they bought every bucket in stock. Then, they went to the tavern and ordered the buckets filled with beer. They drank the stuff right out of pails.

I relaxed and played poker with Gifford, another squad leader and my best friend in the Army.

Giff was a veteran, one of the originals from Maine, and had been wounded in New Georgia. He was five years older than me, and I looked up to him. He was smart and funny and liked the rough outdoor life like I did, and we spent hours trading stories about hunting and fishing. He had a wife, but he rarely mentioned her. I knew his marriage was in trouble when he pulled open his wallet and showed me a picture of his German Shepherd but none of his wife.

Five days after this reverie, July 9, 1944 (my mother's birthday), we marched through the streets of Auckland toward our troop ships anchored in the harbor. By this time, I'd gotten promoted to staff sergeant, three stripes on top, one rocker on bottom. Throngs of cheering spectators lined the street as 3,000 of us in the 103d Infantry Regiment prepared to meet the enemy. I'd waited for this moment for over a year. Still, I was sad to leave Elra. She gave me a parting gift: a second and final kiss.

L Company on a march in New Zealand, June 1944. I'm the seventh back in the near column. Brammer is third from the right. (*Author's collection*)

We boarded an old Norwegian freighter, the S.S. *Torrens*, which would later be sunk by the Japanese. Unlike the reassuring skipper of the *Santa Cruz*, the Norwegian captain of the *Torrens* issued stern warnings about taking our emergency escape drills seriously.

"If vee get hit by torpedo," he said, "vee vill go down in five minutes."

There were no attacks on our ten day voyage to New Guinea, but plenty of the reading, conversing,

The officers of L Company, taken in early 1944 near Warkworth, New Zealand. *Kneeling from left*: Lieutenants Vilano, Fletcher, Ditkoff. *Standing*: Thompson, Dooley, Captain Chase, Foell. Foell and Thompson were killed in action. (*Author's collection*)

and gambling that had kept us busy on our long voyage from the States. There were more poker games than usual, and I seemed to have gotten better at it. By the end of ten days, my pockets were $100 heavier. In tribute to my grandfather Anton Johnson, I donated half of my winnings to the Norwegian War Relief.

On July 19 we arrived at Aitape on the northern

Warkworth, New Zealand, July 4, 1944, Men of 'C' Company, 103rd Infantry, 43rd Division, during long-break on 15 mile march. We left for Aitape, New Guinea July 9.

Our July 4th beer break during our final long march in New Zealand. I'm in the front row, second from the left. My best friend, Giff, is the hatless man to my left. Fraley, the soldier who was sucker punched in a chow line, is back left, holding a bucket of beer. (*Author's collection*)

coast near the center of the giant island of New Guinea. Artillery fire rumbled in the distance. My first sounds of combat. The men on board, especially the new guys, fell a little quiet. What was there to say? "Well, this is it," became the refrain along the railing as we neared the harbor.

We walked ashore with helmets strapped, rifles slung behind us. My field pack bulged with my trenching tool, mess kit, jungle kit, fatigue cap, canteen, razor, and ever-present Bible and Kipling. No enemy fire awaited us at Aitape, no shore masters waving us into battle. Just a couple of GIs, stark naked, taking a walk on the beach.

Fighting had raged on New Guinea almost continuously for two-and-a-half years. We landed in an active sector, where 30,000 members of the Japanese 18th Army, who had somehow subsisted for months on starvation rations, had just nine days earlier launched a massive assault on American lines. The attack was along the Driniumor River, about fifteen miles east of the beachhead of Aitape and the Tadji airstrip. Two battalions of our 169th Regiment deployed to the Driniumor River in support of the 32d Division and the 112th Cavalry Regiment, while my 103d Regiment manned a defensive perimeter closer to the airstrip and harbor. Earlier fighting had high casualties on both sides. The Japanese had charged American machine gun positions in wave after wave. The enemy had achieved several breakthroughs but, exhausted and confused as they were, failed to advance. Our defenses stiffened, and our Air Corps and artillery destroyed thousands of the attackers.

My first night on the perimeter I walked guard duty. The Japanese, we were told, were out there, in the jungle, perhaps watching us. I thought we should have stood guard in foxholes, but there I was, parading along the inside of our line of pill-boxes, bathed in a full moonlight, ears tuned to the noises of the jungle. There were loud and eerie hoots, snorts, and whistles. I heard a rustling in a coconut tree. A Jap sniper, I thought. I raised my rifle. All of a sudden a figure flew silhouetted against the night sky, and I whipped my M1 around to shoot. Past me whooshed a fruit bat with a four-foot wingspan.

We all got used to the jungle noises over the next several weeks as we patrolled through the re-maining Japanese forces in our area. We spent most of our days improving the coconut log pill-boxes that became our new homes. We slept in and on top of them. My hands blistered and grew callused after chopping down coconut trees to create breastworks. One man in my squad, I dis-covered, was even better fitted for this sort of work than I. Charley was from backwoods Alabama and could neither read nor write. Leading him proved a challenge and great management expe-rience. One day, I picked up a heavy log and hoisted it up on my shoulder. Life's too short to hurt myself this way, I thought, and let the log drop. Charley came along, threw it on his shoulder, and walked away. I outweighed him by twenty pounds. By dropping the log, I'd failed to lead by

On New Guinea, we cut down coconut trees to construct our pillboxes. Most men hated this chore. As you can tell from this photo, I loved it. (*Author's collection*)

example. A fellow sergeant saw my consternation and laughed.

"Don't worry about it," the sergeant said. "He's been doing that his whole life. Count yourself lucky if you carry half as much as he does."

Our reinforcement work on the pillboxes saved me from disaster when a squad behind us began test firing 81mm mortars over our heads into the sago swamps beyond the perimeter. Before the shooting began, I decided to stay on top of the pillbox to get a better idea of what those 81mm shells sounded like. I couldn't convince anyone to accompany me on the roof, so I reluctantly joined the rest of my crew inside the bunker. Within seconds of the firing, one mortar fell short and made a direct hit on our pillbox. The explosion damaged the log roof and half buried us in dirt and splinters. We emerged badly shaken and temporarily deafened, but otherwise unhurt. I looked at our shattered roof, my first close call of the war.

On August 15, the 103d Regiment relieved the 32d Division and the 112th Cavalry Regiment on the Driniumor River line where the last Japanese attackers had been killed or scattered into the jungle. We marched in formation with our packs and extra gear toward the front. A putrid odor greeted us before we even reached our destination. Hundreds upon hundreds of dead Japanese in various stages of decay covered the ground by the river line. They were stripped of souvenirs; some were missing ears. Some had swelled to balloon-like proportions, their faces grotesquely distorted, crawling with maggots. Others had begun to show bones. We stepped with care and covered any open cuts or sores to keep out the disease-carrying flies.

These were the first enemy I'd seen, but the impact was largely olfactory. It was hard to get past the odor. We choked back our urge to vomit, and I tried not to show surprise or concern or disgust. "This is it," we mumbled, repeating the refrain we used every time we stepped closer to the real war.

As we marched, I looked over to see a rifleman at work. He'd propped the head of a dead Japanese on a log and was repeatedly bringing his rifle butt down on the corpse's jaw to dislodge some gold teeth. It was none other than the girlish-faced Pfc. Leonard Posey. I frowned on such behavior, but at least Posey had quelled some doubts about himself. You can't judge by appearance, I said to myself. I would learn that lesson again, later on, when the granite-faced staff sergeant Tom De-Lord, who seemed born for combat, was busted back to private after three days on Luzon for his failure to lead.

We manned a foxhole perimeter along the river for a month. Our operations were mostly combat and reconnaissance patrols of eight to fifteen men. Feeling the need to gain experience and prove myself as a leader, I disregarded the old Army adage "never volunteer for anything" and tried to get on as many patrols as possible. Most were short affairs, and I was never able to secure a position on an overnight patrol. But the patrols I did lead proved immensely valuable.

Patrols began with an officer from headquarters meeting with me, telling me the objective, and then opening a map and showing me the route. It might be a "10,000 yard patrol" or longer. Then, I'd call together my patrol and brief them for ten minutes on the assignment. My well-thumbed Army manual on scouting and patrolling emphasized the need for everyone to understand the mission. I was surprised and gratified at the end of one nine-mile patrol when a veteran of New Georgia commented to me, "This was the first time I ever knew why the hell I was out there on patrol. No one had ever really explained our missions before."

We'd head into the jungle carrying a light field pack plus a poncho, a little food, and a few other bare necessities, including an entrenching tool. We packed carefully to make sure our equipment didn't rattle. I was more zealous about silence than other squad leaders and wanted my men to make as little noise as possible. We never had a radio man accompany us, and binoculars weren't much use in the thick cover, but occasionally I'd borrow a pair from an officer. A map and compass were essential in New Guinea. Often the land was flat and almost featureless and the jungle dense. Without these two tools, I'd have gotten lost in twenty minutes. One man in our regiment reportedly headed for a latrine 100 feet from his pillbox and got turned around. It took him twenty-four hours to find his way back.

Shallow sago palm swamps surrounded us. We often patrolled in water, ankle to waist deep, and once remained submerged for five hours. Jungle rot became a problem. A kind of fungus sprouted on your body and clothes after a while. Your fatigues would rot on your back, your service shoes would disintegrate. The slightest dampness in your duffel, and everything was ruined. A scratch or even mosquito bite, if not carefully covered, could get infected. The worst-case scenario was blood poisoning, whose tell-tale signs were red lines radiating up from the wrist. The condition was potentially lethal, and men who got it didn't come back for a long time, if at all.

Shortly after arriving on New Guinea, I spent a couple days slogging in the swamps and didn't remove my boots the whole time. When I finally pulled them off, a layer of skin sloughed off with them. A stomach turning sight, but no pain. After a few days, I noticed my chronic athlete's foot had disappeared entirely. The peel cured me of it.

The jungle made a profound impression on me. Our patrols cut through the thickest vegetation I'd ever seen. Without a trail, we frequently cleared the way with machetes. I counted almost fifty different kinds of vines, all of them with thorns. The Aussie soldiers in New Guinea referred to one variety as the "waitawhile" vine. Once it grabbed you, it seemed to tighten its grip and the more you struggled the more it wrapped around you. Breaking free meant patiently picking away each strand with as little movement as possible.

A whole other world seemed to come alive at night. Lizards, birds, pigs, monkeys all grunted, hummed, chirped, and screamed. The tree canopy exploded with noise. The funny thing was, we rarely saw wildlife, only heard it. Three-toed cassowaries, flightless birds four to five-feet tall and native to the island, left tracks everywhere, but I never got so much as a glimpse of one. Native New Guineans were similarly shy. Whenever we did pass by a village, the people would ignore us completely. Occasionally we'd see a carrying party of natives. Once I glanced over at a native woman at work. One of her pendulous breasts kept getting in the way, so she casually threw it over her shoulder.

The enemy was also elusive and, thanks to our regiment's aggressive patrolling, diminishing in number. My closest encounter with the Japanese on New Guinea came near the end of a nine-mile patrol. We'd followed trails and crossed several streams and then started seeing footprints. Our mission was to locate gun emplacements. There weren't any, but we could tell the Japanese had been there recently. As always, I insisted on silence. We wanted to hear them, I told my men, before they heard us. Most of our squads made too much noise, and I took pride in our stealthy approach.

Two scouts always led our column with me next, right up there with them. As we moved silently up the trail, several of us heard the bolt action of a rifle being worked. It was a Japanese sniper. I turned around and motioned for a couple guys to encircle left and some others to encircle right. I looked at the ground. No mud, only groundcover, and therefore no footprints. We tightened the noose, but our prey escaped the dragnet. We never saw or heard him leave.

If we had surrounded him, I wonder if we'd have been able to take him prisoner. During my entire time on New Guinea, I saw only one live Japanese. We were on a patrol, and a squad ahead of us happened upon a group of enemy soldiers. Instead of even attempting to take them prisoner, this squad simply opened fire and killed all but one, who was badly wounded. I'm guessing these particular enemy soldiers would have surrendered. They were so emaciated they could hardly walk, let alone fight. The lone survivor was a virtual skeleton, stripped down to nothing but a pair of ragged shorts.

Our operations on New Guinea were declared

officially over on August 25. We remained
bivouacked on the Driniumor River and, after a
while, were able to bed down somewhere other
than in our wet foxholes. A buddy and I scrounged
some poles, communication wire, and cardboard
from ration boxes and fashioned makeshift bunks
that rose a couple feet off the ground. We spread a
poncho over us to keep out the rain. This structure
was butted against a fallen tree that was five-feet
in diameter. I slept with the tree brushing my left
shoulder. Before drifting out of consciousness, my
buddy remarked that the tree probably served as a
highway for snakes, lizards, and other things that
crawled in the night. Unwanted creatures were part
of living outdoors, and the Army's SOP (Standard
Operating Procedure) for such visitations was,
"Don't grab them, just let them crawl off."

As I slept, a large snake about two inches in diameter made its way along the windfall tree, then
began to cross on my neck and face, in that order.
I awoke yelling, "SNAKE!" and instinctively threw
it off me. So much for the SOP.

After recovering from paralyzing laughter, my
buddy described what I did next: "It was something physically impossible. You sort of levitated
up off the bunk and then shot out from under the
poncho, feet first, without knocking it down, and
ended standing up."

Such is the exhaustion of combat that within a

few minutes I was back asleep, along the same fallen tree.

In September, we removed to the main perimeter near Aitape to prepare for our next operation, which was rumored to be a beach landing in Formosa or the Philippines. I'd been overseas almost nine months and had neither fired my rifle nor thrown a grenade in anger. We trained to peak condition. One day, after my squad had finished a live fire drill, the instructor chastised me.

"I thought you were such good shots," he said, "but you guys didn't hit a single target."

"Yeah, but look at the trees," I responded. "You won't find an unhit coconut on them." My men had shot every one.

****

My life's moment of greatest terror came toward the end of the New Guinea campaign as I was walking in the dark to our base camp from the Aitape Army Hospital. These were days of mounting anticipation as we trained hard for our next assignment: the long-awaited invasion of Luzon. During one training exercise, we advanced in a squad column while a machine gun fired over our heads in support. As we zigzagged forward, the gun's safety crossbar suddenly slipped, sinking the tripod into the sand and tilting the gun barrel downward at a deadly angle. The bullets narrowly missed me but struck two others, a medic and a corporal named Ames from our headquarters company. I saw Ames fall backward, rushed to his aid, and helped load the bleeding soldier into a jeep. I didn't know him well, but a couple days later I thought I'd pay him the courtesy of a hospital visit.

The shortcut was a two-mile walk on a new and closed gravel road cut through a sago palm swamp. The roadside was thick with vegetation and the jungle animals we so often heard at night. Because the road and hospital fell within our heavily defended perimeter, we weren't permitted to carry rifles. Enemy soldiers occasionally infiltrated, however, and travelling without protection made me tense. I brought along a combat knife, just in case.

I arrived at the hospital and saw Ames who was recovering well from his wounds. But the real delight for me was the man who occupied the next bed, a talkative Australian infantry veteran of the Sicily, North African, and Buna, New Guinea campaigns. Aussie soldiers had reputations as terrific jungle fighters who waged an unforgiving war in defense of their homeland, which was in jeopardy if the Japanese couldn't be stopped on New Guinea. I didn't often encounter these brave Aussies, so I treasured my time with this soldier, who regaled me with stories from Buna, a ferocious battle that took place on New Guinea's southeast tip over two years earlier. He had fought alongside the American 163d Regiment of the 41st Division. The Americans had tried and failed to take a hill from the Japanese. This soldier was among those who swaggered past the static American positions chirping, "We'll take your bloody hill for you, Yank." In the end, the Aussies failed too. Casualties were so great there wasn't anyone left to carry out the wounded until the Americans went in to help.

His other Buna story haunted me. After a rain-soaked night in foxholes, the men charged enemy lines at daybreak and saw three of their own mutilated and hanging on crosses, literally crucified. Wild for vengeance, the Aussies dispatched the Japanese defenders and then happened upon a makeshift jungle hospital with eighty or so wounded Japanese. One of the patients threw a grenade at the Aussies. This broke the tension and unleashed the Aussies' fury. They killed every patient in the hospital, the women too.

Enthralled by the storyteller, I stayed at the hospital longer than I intended, and it was well after dark when I began my trip back to camp. I considered taking the longer route, which had traffic, but decided to return the way I came on that lonely gravel short cut through the swamp.

I walked slowly in pitch blackness. I had no light on this moonless night, except for that given off by a few dim stars. My footsteps crunched and dead palms rustled in the wind. Crazy animal noises rose up all around me, adding to the creepy feeling. I was afraid. The fact that I was alone contributed to the sense of dread. I had no leadership role to play and thus no restraint on my fear.

After about a half an hour, an odd thing happened. I experienced my first episode of extrasensory perception that made the hair on the back of my neck stand on end. I knew something big was about to happen. I stopped, considered turning back, and then thought the better of it. Young soldiers who aspire to courage, I told myself, don't turn back. So I moved forward, cautious and alert.

Suddenly, something large and powerful hit my leg. A storm of squealing, snorting, and thundering hooves erupted around me. Surrounded, I jumped straight into the air and let out a scream of terror. I began trying to battle my way out, running through the encircling forces. After a few steps, I realized what had happened.

A herd of wild pigs had heard me coming and stood motionless in the road until I walked straight into them. Then, they stampeded, and I panicked, stirring up their frenzy even further. The pigs scurried off, and I, again, was left alone. I finished my hike emotionally spent. I'd been feared out.

In telling my buddies about the wild pigs, I remarked that at least now I knew that I wouldn't soil my pants when hugely frightened. I was right. Nothing since has come close to sparking in me that kind of instantaneous high level of fear. The incident was a good conditioner for what was to come.

CHAPTER FOUR

Luzon Beachhead

January 1945

Headquarters officers briefed us with maps and reconnaissance photographs. They instructed us on our objectives and warned that it would be a hot landing. "Expect heavy casualties," they said.

We rehearsed in full gear, trying to mock the intensity of the experience. We disgorged into the water from the great bow jaws of a Landing Ship, Tank (LST—jokingly referred to as "Large Slow Target"), riding in twenty-man loads aboard smaller Amphibious Tractors, also known as Landing Vehicles, Tracked (LVTs) or Amphtracks, which then delivered us to the sand. When the 220 men of L Company boarded an LST for the

A view from a deck of an LST on the Lingayen Gulf invasion. (*U.S. Navy, National Archives*)

real journey north to Luzon, we each had a good idea of what we were getting into.

We departed from New Guinea three days after Christmas and joined an enormous convoy of vessels, 1,200 in all, that made the Luzon invasion the biggest of the Pacific war. Although it was my fourth ocean-borne journey as an Army sergeant, this trip was different. There were the books and card games, the bull sessions and the gambling, but the feel and smell of war surrounded us like never before. The LST was packed, absolutely jammed, on deck and below, with every sort of gun, truck, and piece of Army equipment imaginable. It was

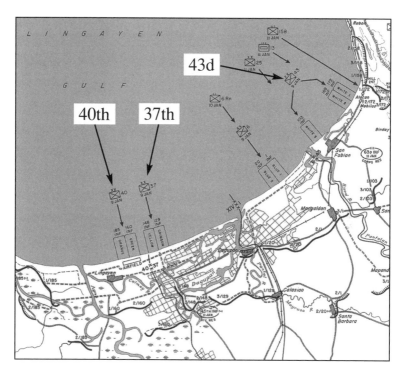

Map of the Lingayen Gulf Invasion, January 9, 1945. Arrows show position of the 37th, 40th and 43d Divisions on the evening of 11 Jan 1945. (*U.S. Army, Department of Defense*)

as if the ship was loaded to the gunwales and then, as an afterthought, L Company was piled on top. Every square foot of space was taken, and we picked our way through the olive drab cargo to find a truck seat or open sliver of deck. Center poles were erected and hammocks strung up over the clutter.

We approached the southern Philippine islands and heard the distant rumble of antiaircraft guns.

We could barely make out Japanese airplanes attacking the head of the convoy. These were some of the early kamikaze missions of the war. "This is it," came the now familiar refrain. As we neared the Lingayen Gulf, our destination, a kamikaze appeared two hundred yards off port from the rear. I ran to the railing. I had pictured kamikazes attacking at steep angles, but this one approached at thirty degrees as it hurtled straight toward a neighboring LST carrying our regiment's I Company. I thought about our ship. Many of the "deuce-and-a-half" trucks on board were loaded with TNT. Even a small bomb, let alone a kamikaze, would blow us all into a billion pieces.

We watched the action along the rail like spectators at a football game. "Get 'im, get 'im!" we yelled as every antiaircraft gun in the vicinity unloaded on the doomed kamikaze. The plane began shedding parts, and finally a wing tore off as it somersaulted into the water. By the time it hit about 100 yards from its LST target, the airplane had smashed into so many bits that the wreckage wasn't even visible. We cheered in triumph.

Our shouts turned to moans when the gunners, carried away by their zeal, continued firing after the plane had crashed. Many bullets slammed into the LST carrying I Company, achieving some of the damage that the kamikaze had failed to inflict.

I Company suffered eleven casualties from those guns. We turned away from the railing shaking our heads. Soon, we'd mentally accommodate ourselves to friendly fire, as we did to many repugnant things, in order to stay sane.

Rain fell as we approached the Lingayen Gulf. Ahead of us, Seventh Fleet battleships, cruisers, and destroyers began shelling enemy installations while mine sweepers cleared a channel. Our LST churned west under dark clouds and passed small islands on each side. Late in the day, the rain stopped and the sky slowly opened up revealing streaks of yellow light. We were sailing directly into a sunset.

As the rays burst through, a swath of gold enveloped the clouds on either side of the sun. Violent reds and purples appeared, then mellowed into pinks and magentas and grays, and then changed back. The cycle repeated itself over and over, spreading outward from the sun. Our ship bobbed and swayed gently beneath this kaleidoscope of color. Soldiers and sailors on deck put down their cards and dice and moved to the railing. More men emerged from below deck. It's a mighty testament indeed to the awe the display inspired that all gambling and most conversations aboard our LST came to a halt. Voices were hushed, except for an occasional "wow."

The colors bled into the remaining white clouds, inching by degrees until they filled most of the sky. Time passed, and the colors only deepened as they spread. "It can't get any better this," someone remarked. But it did, second by second for over an hour. Finally, in the closing minutes, 360 degrees of splendor. No one aboard that ship would ever experience anything like it again. War brings forth the obscene and repulsive but, in so doing, heightens one's appreciation of beauty. The sunset had broken up every dice and card game on the ship.

A couple days later, we turned toward the gulf. The naval bombardment and sweeping progressed toward our landing areas, and underwater demolition teams reconnoitered the beaches. At 0700 on January 9, 1945—our D-Day—Navy guns began pounding the shore. The air-quivering booms escalated over the next two-and-a-half hours as we descended down steel ladders into the cavernous hold of the LST filled with the rumbling engines of seventeen Amphtracks. Giant forced air ventilators sucked the exhaust fumes through the roof and out the deck vents. My squad of fourteen, two more than usual due to the expected high casualties, found its assigned Amphtrack and settled in. The bow doors of the LST opened, and a ramp dropped like a dragon's tongue into the water. The Amphtracks backed down the incline, one by one, and circled until all had debarked. Anyone watching from above would have seen great whitewater cloverleaves forming and then breaking up as the first waves made their way toward the beach.

I looked around at my men and saw some fear, but a few appeared to be feeling only what I did: alertness, tension, excitement, and no fear. It bothered me a little that I wasn't scared. Was that normal? Was I not appreciative enough of the danger? I maintained a kind of clinical detachment that kept me focused on the job.

Our first objective was to disable any Japanese pillboxes we encountered on the beach and then move inland. I turned over in my mind what kind of a wound it was going to take to put me out of action. I decided that I would try and keep going except for a compound wound with bones showing.

Rumors of stiff Japanese resistance on the beach had multiplied during our LST journey. One squad leader reported that an officer on board had told him to expect sixty percent casualties upon landing. I had my doubts about this. From reading the papers about the invasion of Peleliu a few months earlier, I suspected that the Japanese were shifting their defensive tactics away from all-out assaults on the shoreline. On Peleliu, the enemy moved their fortifications inland, allowed the 1st

First-wave soldiers from my 103rd Regiment wade through a stream en route to San Fabian on the morning of January 9, 1945. (*U.S. Army, Department of Defense*)

Marine Division to land, and then challenged the American invaders to evict them from caves, bunkers, and underground positions.

I shared these thoughts with my squad and burned with curiosity to see if they were accurate. We weren't supposed to peer over the sides of the Amphtrack, but I couldn't resist. Straining for a clear view, I caught sight of the beach. No gun fire, no men sprawled in the sand, no mortars exploding. My suspicions were confirmed. The landing wouldn't be hot. We'd be fighting them inland.

The Amphtrack ground to shore and let down its ramp on White Beach 3 adjacent to the town of San Fabian. It was 0940. We clambered off and instantly sank into the fine sand. I was in the best shape of my life, yet the seventy-pound load I was carrying made it difficult for me to move forward. I had four bandoliers of ammunition, plus a clip in my rifle, three or four grenades, three days' worth of K-rations, water-filled canteens, a bazooka shell which weighed several pounds, and a couple of 60mm mortar rounds. We were all packing too much and would quickly learn to shed what we didn't need.

Our immediate objective was to charge 100 to 200 yards up the beach and attack enemy pillboxes. There were none, so we entered battered San Fabian, which was still smoldering from the shelling of our Navy guns. The only dead we saw were Filipino. Wails of grief from mothers and wives drifted in the air with the smoke.

If we had heeded the advance intelligence Filipino guerrillas had given us, we would've known that the Japanese had retreated from San Fabian to a complex of low grassy hills several miles to the north and east. In the coming weeks, we would get to know these hills, each of which received a numerical designation on Army charts. Hill 200 would be our company's first, and we passed through San Fabian's rubble and started down the San Jacinto road in order to get there.

The primary objective of the invasion was Manila, which lay 120 miles to the south. The Lingayen Gulf operation was a back door approach to the capital, a longer but far easier line of attack than attempting to land a force on the shores of Manila Bay, which the Japanese had heavily fortified. From our location, the road to Manila was flanked by high ground on either side, and we would have to either bypass or secure those positions in order to move forward.

Up ahead I could hear enemy artillery booming. As part of the second wave, sent ten minutes after the first, we didn't receive the brunt of the initial Japanese resistance. As it happened, the enemy was concentrated not in our White Beach 3 sector but on our division's left, where the 169th and 172d Regiments were taking heavy casualties. Despite our easy going, evidence of the danger hit home a half mile up the road as our squad filed past a dead American soldier. He was the first I'd seen killed in action. The man's face was partially covered, but I recognized him as a lieutenant from battalion headquarters who'd once given me instruction in chemical warfare. I thought it dumb to let him lay there as a signpost of battle. We each glanced down at him and looked over his crumpled jeep, which had been hit by artillery. "This is it."

Artillery began hitting closer to us as we made our way toward the town of San Jacinto. The Japanese occupied artillery positions created by the Americans before the war and registered their fire on intersections and bottlenecks where it could do maximum damage. At the same time, our own artillery fired from ships sailed over our heads the other way, and I listened carefully for the distinction. I wanted to learn how to judge distance and direction.

Sound magnitude was a function of caliber and distance. The bigger the shell, the louder the sound. Huge projectiles like railroad artillery and big guns on ships sound like freight trains. Mortars had more of a muffled *thump-thump* than artillery and was sometimes preceded by the pop of the round hitting the boom of the tube, but followed by a brief *sssshhhhh* of the descending shell. Distant artillery was a sustained rumble. Some flying shells had a low-pitched whistle or whooshing sound that I soon figured out meant they were still too far away to be a threat. I hadn't heard dangerously close artillery…yet.

War was now a lesson in sound. There was so much of it all around, all the time. Explosions and shouts, rifles and engines. Some sounds signaled danger, others not. The gap between what I knew and what I needed to learn was becoming obvious, and I kept alert, taking in all I could.

Late in the afternoon that first day, our company commander gave orders to dig foxholes in a peanut field northwest of San Jacinto. The digging was mercifully easy, but the guard duty we pulled that night sitting in foxholes was the worst kind: one hour on, one hour off. The reasoning was that no man could stay awake longer than an hour, but it meant that we never got more than an hour's sleep at a time. Over the coming weeks, when it was my turn to sleep, I would sometimes begin a prayer only to be shaken awake before I'd even finished. I'd protest in vain to my partner that the hour hadn't passed and that I hadn't slept. More merciful and common was guard duty shared with another foxhole, which meant one or two hours on and three times that off.

In my foxhole that first night was Frank Fecser, son of Hungarian immigrants who handled our platoon's flamethrower, a truly terrifying weapon. We talked little, except to share our appreciation for the day's light action. We knew the Japanese were out there close by, and were also aware of their penchant for night attacks. The night seemed to last forever as I peered out into the blackness looking for signs of the enemy while artillery exploded everywhere but on top of us.

The whistle or whish of high artillery travelling safely at a distance was replaced by the louder wolf's cries of shells sailing closer to us, but still not threatening immediate harm. Each time, the cry would grow louder as the shell approached, and my stomach would tighten until the sound began to fade.

We soon learned that whenever one of our artillery spotting aircraft appeared overhead, the enemy stopped firing. The Japanese didn't want our Piper cubs to locate their guns, so they kept quiet until the plane left. I later heard how many of our spotter pilots, knowing the relief they gave us, remained aloft until they were nearly out of fuel. They put themselves in danger just to make our lives a little easier. That's the kind of valor I got to know on Luzon.

Either that night or one soon after, I saw silhouetted against the moonlight what looked to be a Japanese saber raised in the air not more than a few yards away. I snapped around and was about to shoot when the outline of a larger form emerged connected to the sword. It was an enormous water buffalo, or carabao, which had silently wandered into our lines. The saber was the carabao's horn. Accidental shootings of these ubiquitous beasts would unfortunately become common occurrences during our time on Luzon.

Men continued to land and crowd the beachhead on the morning of January 10. Soon, there would be 175,000 of us on Luzon, and the dust clouds whipped up by all those tracks, tires, and marching boots gave the dawn a sepia hue. Still in our foxholes, we heard the sound of machine guns overhead. It was a Navy F-6F fighter hot on the tail of a Japanese Zero. The damaged Zero careened to the ground a couple hundred yards away, and we let out a muted cheer. Our enthusiasm for such spectacles had diminished a bit now that we were on land, in the thick of it ourselves.

We marched down a dusty gravel road past the town of Manaoag to the grassy western slopes of Hill 200, where 600 Japanese soldiers had dug bunkers, tunnels, and machine gun emplacements. They also had fifteen artillery pieces, some of them pulled by horses or tractors. These tormented us. More wolf's cries than whistles now, and they were louder than ever. Incoming shells registered a higher pitch—*eeeee!*—than outgoing ones—*oooooh!*—due to the Doppler Effect, which added the speed of sound to the velocity of the projectile. My stomach tightened with each *eeeee* and loosened with each *ooooh.* Inevitably, the *oooohs* collapsed to danger-ously short intervals.

Then, I clearly heard a 75mm or 77mm artillery shell let out a sustained *eeee* but no *ooooh* to signal the all clear. The explosion sounded like a metallic tearing or cracking sound, a sickening scream that no one who has heard it can ever for-get. Your instinct is to run and seek cover, the proper response to machine gun fire. But with ar-tillery or mortars, you have to fight that instinct and drop in place, getting as close to the ground as you can.

This first artillery barrage was a new and terri-fying sensation that defies easy description. You feel small and helpless, a pure victim to larger forces that are ripping your foothold from the earth. No caution, cunning, courage, or training can help you. There's no fighting back. You lie on the ground face down, hands over your helmet, waiting for it to stop, but the cries, shrieks, and cracking keep coming with a volume that's literally deafening. In truth, these attacks usually last only a few minutes, but time stretches out when solid ground seems to rise and retract, smashing your solar plexus over and over, knocking the wind out of you. Were my ears bleeding? Would I lose con-sciousness? Then, it's over. You pick yourself up and, if not wounded, stagger down the road, a bit more shaken and wary than before.

The next several days were a blur of marching and digging, advancing and maneuvering, between Hill 200 and the critical road juncture at the town of Pozorrubio. This was a frustrating time for me. For one thing, we rarely saw the enemy. I was in battle on Luzon four days before I spotted Japanese soldiers in action. They were running along a ridge line, perhaps 300 yards away, and I didn't shoot because I was unsure of our orders. Sometimes we were supposed to ignore the enemy so as not to give away our positions as we tried to bypass the bunkers and caves. But other times it seemed sensible to fire. I was several days on the ground before I started behaving like the rifleman I was trained to be.

Our artillery batteries too were stingy with their firing. The Japanese were well supplied. We weren't. With limited ammunition, we could only call in fire after we'd visually confirmed the location of an enemy gun. Determining the position by sound or muzzle smoke wasn't good enough. Consequently, we couldn't fight back much. We took a lot of fire and dished out little in those early days.

Things changed dramatically at the end of our first week when the Japanese retreated from Hill 200 and Pozorrubio and established a new line of defense along Route 3, a north-south highway abutting a mass of ridges to the east. Again, each hill had a number, ranging from Hill 600 in our zone to Hill 1500 six miles north. Thirteen thousand Japanese defenders were burrowed on this line in an attempt to prevent us from establishing our beachhead and moving south on Manila. The gentle dusty slopes of Hill 200 gave way to steeper more forbidding terrain as we crossed Route 3. A series of crowded peaks worked their way north, separated by deep draws and often covered with thick stands of bamboo. We had little knowledge of enemy troop dispositions. We were unaware of just how elaborate the Japanese defenses were. Caves concealed artillery, mortars, and infantry, and tunnels connected the caves. Our division commander, General Wing, ordered frontal assaults on this six-mile line on January 19.

That was the day we moved up the southern slope of Hill 600. We charged over land that was scrubby and bare with almost no cover. Behind us, artillery batteries launched shell after booming shell on Japanese positions uphill, while Sherman tanks, one per squad, idled in front us, waiting for the barrage to lift. Such European Theater-style armored assaults were unusual in the Pacific, and they weren't to my liking. All the guns that mattered were the big ones, which I didn't shoot. They

boomed while we riflemen hunkered down, fourteen of us lying in the dust behind our Sherman
tank. While the ground shook around us, I removed my Bible from my pack. I turned to the
91st Psalm for comfort: "His truth shall be thy
shield...A thousand shall fall at thy side, and ten
thousand at thy right hand; but it shall not come
nigh thee...." Looking up, I saw that the four men
closest to me had their Bibles out also.

We couldn't see the enemy, but since they held
the high ground, we were pretty sure they could
see us. I ordered my men to spread out like we
were taught so as not to attract fire. In the movies,
soldiers are always bunched, because they have to
fit in the camera frame and deliver lines to each
other. In real life, such groupings make big fat
targets for the enemy who like to launch missiles
at them and score several kills with one blast.

We lay motionless on the bald hillside. Across a
shallow valley, I saw a soldier from another company
pick himself up, walk over, and flop down next to a
second man. He was probably scared and wanted
company. "Don't ever do that!" I yelled to my squad,
pointing across the valley. "They're just asking for
it." Incredibly, a third man joined the pair. It was
only a matter of time. Within seconds—POW!—
a knee mortar round landed right in their midst.
They were all hit. If lucky, just wounded. My men

watched in silence, adding this to the stock of lessons they were rapidly acquiring.

The bombardment ended, our cue to advance up the hill. Again, we held our fire. As we got closer to enemy lines, the Japanese unloaded a tremendous knee-mortar barrage on top of us. The smoke and dust cleared, and it seemed like half my squad had disappeared. Only three, it turned out, were wounded. My squad's first.

We were completely exposed on that dry southern slope of Hill 600, and only had our foxholes to protect us. The artillery barrages were relentless, and they shook me up almost every time. During one attack, my stomach tightened as I listened for the fading *oooooh*. It never came, and the shell exploded with a metallic tearing sound not four feet away from me. The concussion threw me in the air and dropped me hard. I was convinced my right leg had been severely hit, and I felt down to check the damage. My leg was in tact, but there was some blood where a piece of shrapnel had ripped into my calf. The medic who treated the wound offered me a Purple Heart, but I shook my head.

"Save it for the guys who really deserve it," I said.

Guys like Ed Kozarek, whose birthday was that very day, got a good present, fragment wounds in his leg and foot that might get him home.

In retrospect, perhaps I should have taken the medal. With the heat and dirt, my small wound got infected and plagued me for weeks.

For three days and three nights we held our ground on Hill 600 against heavy enemy artillery. Then, an act of almost unimaginable carelessness thwarted the entire operation. I witnessed the whole thing from 300 yards away. It was an unusually quiet morning. No Japanese artillery. Officers from our 3d battalion, including my own L Company commander, assembled for a meeting. They were in full view of the enemy. The official Army history, *Triumph in the Philippines*, tells what happened next:

> An incautious grouping of officers and enlisted men in the open at a forward command post on Hill 600's southern slopes brought down fifteen well-placed rounds of Japanese 75mm. artillery fire. Within minutes four company commanders were killed and two others officers were wounded; seven enlisted men were killed and thirty-three more were wounded, many of them key NCOs.

Trees and a rock wall combined to spread the fragments lethally. I heard the repeated cry

"Medic!" and ran to a nearby unit.

"Grab all the litters you have," I yelled. "They'll need 'em."

Word came back that our company commander was one of the killed.

We withdrew from Hill 600 to reorganize the battalion and revamp our plan of attack. Within a couple days, we were back on the hill, this time advancing up its grassy western slopes. Machine gun and rifle fire signaled we were getting closer to the enemy. Suddenly, out of the corner of my eye, I spotted two Japanese running with a machine gun along the ridgetop about 300 yards away. I estimated the ballistics and tried judge whether I had a shot. I hesitated, and my targets disappeared. Another first shot lost.

I didn't have to wait long for another chance. It was at night, and we were dug in. The Japanese began shouting at us. We couldn't understand the words but instinctively knew their meaning, and we responded in kind.

"Come and get it you yellow cocksuckers!"

I was antsy, anxious for action and curious about the enemy's position.

"I'm going to scout things out over there," I told my squad, pointing east, toward the voices. I climbed out of my foxhole and walked carefully along the ridge, my rifle made steady by a hasty sling. About 150 yards away, a Japanese soldier jumped out of a foxhole and started running. I raised my M1 and squeezed off a good shot. I didn't see him fall, but I had the feeling I might have gotten him.

My eagerness for experience, to learn more, remained boundless, even after two weeks of combat. A couple days after that first shot, I heard some fire at the other end of our company's line and suggested to our leader, platoon sergeant Loren McAllister, that I go check it out. I arrived in time to witness Gifford, my old buddy from New Zealand who carried a photo of his German Shepherd in his wallet, loaded on to a litter. A mortar shell had gotten Giff in the neck. He was still alive but covered in blood from head to toe. I walked back to our platoon shaken by what I'd seen.

That same day just before dark, L Company lost communication with battalion. The radios weren't working, and the phone wire was cut. I was ordered to take my squad and fix the cut wire at daylight.

I knew the Japanese liked to sever telephone lines and then ambush repair crews. We followed the wire across one of the many rice paddies set among the folds of Hill 600. As evening came on, we stopped to dig foxholes. It was the worst digging we'd encountered, no soil at all, just flaked rock. We all gave up and simply piled stones around us like little castle walls. When not on guard duty, my partner and I slept fitfully in the fetal position surrounded by rocks.

At first light, I saw a Japanese soldier at fifty yards running away from us. I took a fast shot before he disappeared. Again, I didn't know if I got him, and that bothered me a little. We braced ourselves for the ambush that never came. Our communications specialists found the cut, spliced the wires, and we returned to our platoon without incident.

The next day, someone told me Giff was dead. The news hit me hard. Unlike most veterans of the first New Guinea campaign, Giff welcomed combat, despite already having a Purple Heart. In New Zealand, we'd sometimes joked about his idea of serving together as mercenaries in South America after the war. I thought about his orphaned German Shepherd. Poor Giff.

I might have taken Giff's death more in stride if my defenses hadn't been broken down by living in foxholes for over two weeks. After sleeping only a couple hours a night for days on end, my fatigue was profound. To top it off, I had a bad case of dysentery. I staggered through that day—the day I heard of Giff's death—in a fog of bad morale, the worst I experienced. I remember looking at some dead men lying on the ground and thinking they might have a better deal. I stubbornly clung to my role as leader, however, and refused to betray my feelings.

The constant artillery barrages were also wearing me down, and on my bad morale day, I found myself caught in the open when shells began exploding around me. I ran a short distance and dove for cover in small dry creek bed, one of many that wound through the hills of Luzon. Suddenly, from a few yards away, came a loud and joyous, not-a-care-in-world greeting.

"Hey, Jay, great to see ya! How've ya been?"

It was the hulking Louis Magrames from Mishiwaka, Indiana, the soldier who had spoken cryptically of his grudge against the Japanese. Here he was, utterly indifferent to ground-shaking explosions, as chirpy and chippy as if we had run into each other on a train. Earlier that week, I heard that Magrames twice had found an enemy soldier in a foxhole, stuck him with a bayonet, and then lifted him clear out of the hole. This was a man who clearly exalted in combat. His attitude buoyed my spirits immediately, and I told him, without lying, that everything was just right.

As for Giff, I later received the good news that he had in fact survived his neck wound and would soon be returning to action. He did come back a couple of months later, but he didn't last long. After I'd left L Company for my new platoon, I got the news that Giff had been killed by friendly fire. An American 155mm shell had landed on top of him. There was nothing left to bury. Perhaps it's a testament to how my encounter with Magrames inoculated me against future bad morale days that when I learned of Giff's real death I took note of it in sorrow and carried on with my duties in my usual high spirits.

The Japanese pulled some of their troops from Hill 600 and put them in dugout positions on similar hills further back from our beachhead line. We worked increasingly with Filipino guerrillas, who were uneven in quality as soldiers. One day, I was given a squad of fifteen guerrillas and told to go with them to intercept some Filipino refugees coming from behind Japanese lines. My scouts were elsewhere that day, so I patrolled up front with a guerrilla sergeant as partner. We tracked a dry creek bed toward the rendezvous point where we were to meet the refugees. Up ahead of us, I saw a large brush pile like a beaver dam blocking our path. Footprints in the creek bed suggested that the brush pile was man made.

"The Japs are around here," I told the guerrilla. "That brush pile is fresh. They're trying to divert us into an ambush."

The Filipino sergeant waved off my concern and charged ahead up the bank around the brush pile.

Soon after he disappeared from view, we heard a shot. The sergeant stumbled back gripping a bloody wrist. I turned to see that all the guerrillas had left. I stepped up toward the brush pile and, looking beyond it, could see some shadow figures. I lifted my rifle and squeezed off three or four rounds at 100 yards. Once again, I walked away not knowing if I scored a kill. The first men I saw as we retreated were in my squad.

We were put into battalion reserve for forty-eight hours. We dug foxholes in a coconut grove just outside of Pozurrubio. The rest was welcome and lifted our spirits.

On the second day, Filipino civilians came to our command post and said that three Japanese had been spotted on the edge of town. Knowing what we'd been through recently, the company commander just called for volunteers to find these enemy soldiers. He found ten of us willing to go.

Accompanying me was Chalmus Brammer, the tall, baby-faced, happy-go-lucky young Texan I'd befriended in New Guinea. Bram was a first scout in another squad, and I liked being paired with someone who was accustomed to being up front, alert, and stealthy.

As usual, it was sticky hot. The wet ground and foliage from the rain the night before allowed us to move quietly. After about an hour of searching, the other eight soldiers gave up to look for some eggs in a nearby village. We'd been on canned and boxed rations for a couple of weeks and were starved for fresh food. But Bram and I kept at it. We had a sense the Japanese were out here somewhere.

We were moving silently in the same direction about fifty yards apart when I found fresh tracks made by a pair of *jikatabi*, the distinctive Japanese split-toed shoes. I kept in mind that sometimes the Filipinos scrounged these shoes from the Japanese, living or dead, and wore them around. My dad's advice came to me: "C and C, Caution and Cunning. Always keep thinking."

I followed the prints along one side of an elevated square of foot high grass bordered by banana trees. This twenty-five-yard-by-twenty-five-yard area was raised about three feet above two adjoining rice paddies. The paddies were on two adjacent sides of the square. The other two sides merged with the land at the same elevation as the grassy plot.

When I reached the corner of the elevated area and entered the rice paddy, I could see that the tracks turned at a right angle and headed to the next corner twenty-five yards away. This made me cautious. If I continued to follow the tracks, I might turn the corner and be face to face with enemy soldiers. So, instead of following the foot-prints, I walked straight out into the watery paddy, which was flat and had little vegetation, offering a clear line of sight.

About thirty yards into the paddy away from the square, I turned and looked back at the corner where the tracks struck a right angle. Something didn't seem right. I didn't know what it was, but it wasn't right. So I retraced my steps and then, crouching low, ascended the grassy square and crept across it. I was on the center line of the elevated tract headed to where it joined the rice paddy on the side I hadn't seen.

Approaching the banana tree border, I tensed up, and the hair on the back of my neck bristled, just like on the gravel road with the wild pigs in New Guinea. I knew something big was about to happen.

I peered over the edge of the square. Ten feet away from me at the edge of the paddy was a Japanese soldier. His back was to me. His head was about level with my knees, and he held the barrel of his rifle in his extended right hand with the butt on the ground. He was gazing out over the rice paddy. Perhaps he was thinking of home.

I looked at the back of his head through the peep sight of my M1. Our men sometimes wore Japanese equipment—though I'd never seen anyone with an enemy helmet—so I didn't shoot. Could this really be a knotheaded ally dressed like a Jap? I asked myself.

As I hesitated, a whistle cried out from behind. It was Brammer signaling me. I kept my right eye locked in the sight as the enemy soldier turned his head toward the whistle. His profile showed he was Japanese. I squeezed the trigger and shot him in the head. He plunged forward.

Voices and the rattle of equipment below told me he wasn't alone. I dropped back from the edge about five steps and pulled the pin on my only hand grenade. I let the lever go, counted two-plus seconds and lobbed the grenade toward the noise. It exploded, and I heard a groan.

Bram approached.

"I got two," I told him, "and there's at least one left, maybe more than that."

Bram didn't have any grenades, so we moved out into the paddy. I led and Bram followed twelve feet behind. We tiptoed through three inches of water. We heard the sound of a grenade pop, which meant an explosion would be coming in five seconds. We knelt down and briefly bowed our heads.

The grenade went off, and a body rose up out of the tall weeds at the edge of the paddy. It turned end over end like a rag doll and flopped to the ground—a suicide. We began firing rapidly at a range of about forty feet. The remaining Japanese threw a couple of ineffectual grenades that exploded in the water, delivering showy columns of mud but failing to blow outward. They fired at us through heavy screens of weeds and rice, and we did the same at them. It was a frenzy of fire, and Bram was as excited as I.

"Hey, Jay, this is all right!" he yelled as he pulled his trigger. "Just like the movies!"

Even in the euphoria of battle, Bram and I coordinated our shots so that we never had two empty clips at a time. Each clip held eight rounds, and we counted out loud as we fired.

"Three to go!"

We kept up our attack as the enemy fire dwindled and then dropped to almost zero. Bram moved in close until he was about ten feet away from them and resumed rapid fire.

"There are a lot of them!" he shouted, using the proper grammar.

I advanced toward the other end of their position, getting close like Bram. Someone moved. I shot him. We fired a few more rounds for good measure, and it was all over.

Nine Japanese lay dead, most of them touching one another. If all seven survivors of my first shot and the grenade had stood up together, Bram and I might have been the dead ones.

A shout came across the rice paddy. The eight other men from our patrol, having found their eggs, approached in a skirmish line, weapons ready.

Neither Bram nor I spent much time looking for souvenirs or intelligence information (the usual order of body searches). I grabbed a saber and looked down at the nine people we'd just killed. It wasn't a pleasant sight. But I was impressed by the lack of blood. Then I noticed near the corner of the raised area a leather ammunition pouch. That was it. Light reflecting off the pouch was what seemed out of place when I first looked this way from out in the paddy.

I felt my shirt front which had two clips attached and calculated that I'd fired nearly 100 rounds like Bram. Bram later told me that when battalion headquarters heard the furious firing, they considered sending tank support.

We left the rest of the cleanup to the eight others and returned to the coconut grove where our platoon was getting ready to pull out for another go at Hill 600. As we marched, I relayed the tale of the day's events to my squad. One guy remarked, "I'd rather be lucky than smart."

He was right, but I grew smarter in the coming weeks. If this had happened at the end of February instead of in January, I'd have fired the first shot, thrown the grenade, and then run for help.

****

The remaining enemy on Hill 600 proved stubbornly resistant to eviction. We probed the area for defensive installations that our Air Corps and artillery batteries could strike.

The official history explains that we made limited use of air power in partially clearing Hills 600-1500. What it doesn't say is how during the last week of January the Air Corps decimated our 103d Regiment with friendly fire.

By this time, the Japanese were deep in their caves, and we had launched patrols to root them out. As daylight broke, we watched from the base of Hill 600 as C Company of the 1st battalion ascended for the grim task of blowing up caves. Suddenly, over head, roared waves of P-51 Mustang fighters and A-20 light bombers. The fighters strafed the hilltop with 50 caliber machine guns, shooting up C Company. Their spent shells dropped on us like hot coins from heaven. The A-20s, meanwhile, torched the ridgeline with a new invention: napalm, a terrifying anti-personnel weapon made of jellied gasoline. Other planes dropped parachuted anti-personnel bombs. Fiery balls billowed from C Company's position as we gaped in helpless horror. Several of my men openly cried and screamed at the pilots to stop.

"You're shooting the wrong guys, you stupid fucks!"

One soldier raised his rifle and began firing at the airplanes. Others followed suit, directing their rage at the ignorant perpetrators. I ran up and down the line yelling at my men and knocking down their weapons. After a few passes, I got the squad under control. We all stood numb cursing as the planes flew off, oblivious to the carnage they'd inflicted. I thought of the Army slang term I'd learned in training: FUBAR—Fucked Up Beyond All Recognition.

The next day, we stirred to life and packed up for a patrol. We still had to take Hill 600. No one said a word about the friendly fire. It was like it never happened. We'd settled in to the world of combat, where the rule of life is one day, one hour, one step at a time. There was always plenty of danger and FUBAR ahead. No need to dwell on what was behind.

Still, that incident rankled, even if we couldn't speak of its impact. Its memory lodged somewhere in our exhausted brains, registering in that primitive part that senses doom and responds accordingly. Down deep, each of us woke up wondering, "How can I survive this? Even my own side is against me." We knew it wasn't intentional, but the war now seemed more frighteningly unpredictable. We took a turn toward crazy, and the stresses of battle began to show in funny ways.

We were assigned lead platoon on a long hot patrol on the far side of Hill 600. As we crossed a rice paddy, the air crackled with the sound of rifle and machine gun fire. We dropped face down into the paddy and hid in the narrow drainage ditches. I stuck my head up to get a sense of the fire source and my right ear suddenly went deaf. A bullet had passed close, maybe a quarter inch away from my head. It would take two days for my hearing to return.

Pinned down in a field of shallow water, I looked sideways and saw our platoon leader, Loren McAllister, walking casually through the paddy carrying his rifle at the balance like he was hunting deer.

"For God's sakes, Mac, get down!" I yelled.

Mac dropped next to me as bullets smacked the mud around him.

Mac's nonplussed attitude, his coolness under fire, made a deep impression on me. He was one of the originals from Maine, in the Army for three years, a veteran of the first New Georgia campaign, and a hell of a soldier and leader. At age twenty-six, he was like a much-admired big brother. That he turned to me in the rice paddy to coordinate our withdrawal signaled his respect for my soldiering, and I reveled in it.

"We're sitting ducks, Mac," I told him. "Let's cover the men as they crawl out of here."

With Mac and me firing, every man in our platoon made it safely to a paddy dike, a bank of earth that shielded them from bullets. Finally, it was our turn to get out.

"It's so damn hot, Grunie, let's make a run for it," Mac said gamely.

How could I say no?

At the count of three we jumped up and ran full speed as the machine guns opened fire, striking everything, it seemed, but us. Full of demented bravado, I shouted obscenities in defiance.

"Shoot, you cocksuckers, shoot!"

We arrived at the dike and dove for cover. The men, clearly disturbed by this display, greeted us with open jaws and looks of concern. I'd never felt better.

That rush of adrenaline kept me steady when, a few minutes later, the Japanese responded to our successful withdrawal by lobbing mortars at us. Artillery comes in at an angle, but mortars drop straight down. There's almost nothing you can do to defend yourself, and the feeling is normally terrifying. I stayed cool, along with Mac, and watched in pity as some of our men panicked. One soldier furiously burrowed into the dike, clawing the earth with his bare hands.

Our next patrol continued up and down hills and across more paddies. Again, we got pinned down by a machine gun in a forward position, and again we had to withdraw across a paddy to safety.

One of the first to run for it was Private Robert Garmany from Anniston, Alabama. If looks counted in soldiering, Garmany would have flunked out. He always had something wrong with his uniform. A shirt tail flapping, steel helmet crooked, pant legs drooped over his leggings. He was a cut-up, and his slow drawl made everything he said sound funny. But the biggest laugh he ever got was on this sprint for cover, and no humor was intended.

Garmany, we discovered, had a funny loping gallop with flopping elbows made all the more hilarious by the machine gun rounds that chased him across the rice paddy. The bullets matched his crazy strides step for step, but they couldn't hit Garmany's flailing legs. In our semi-psychotic state, we laughed uproariously as the rounds landed just in front, just in back, and then actually between the flapping pant legs of this desperate soldier. We cheered when Garmany made it to the dike, almost forgetting that we too were under fire.

A little batty from the weeks of combat and feeling somewhat invincible, I concluded our platoon's withdrawal by consciously emulating Mac. When it was my turn to head down the hill and across the paddy, I did so walking, not running. I made my way with deliberate nonchalance so that my men could see me and be inspired. It was perhaps the dumbest thing I ever did, which is saying something.

Playing the role of fearless leader is important, but too much of it can get you killed.

****

After we had been in heavy combat on Luzon for about a month, we had a quiet period and were able to have a bull session where almost the whole squad, by then maybe seven or eight men left out of fourteen, joined in. We talked about the sometime problem of determining how aggressive you should be in an attack. There were questions such as where to draw the line between being cautious and being cowardly and where courage became stupidity. Garm brought the house down when he said in his slow drawl, "Well I know one thing. When we are in the attack and there is a man behind me, I call that man a coward."

Standing atop Hill 600 in January 1995. This is where our Air Corps napalmed C Company, blowing them off the hill, after we'd suffered so many casualties to take it. Down below are the rice paddies where I courted danger to impress my men and where we laughed as machine gun bullets struck in between the legs of Garmany. (*Author's collection*)

CHAPTER FIVE

Commissioned in Battle

February-March 1945

In early February, a Filipino civilian came to our outpost and reported seeing three enemy soldiers enter a sugarcane field on the outskirts of town. Ten of us volunteered to go find them.

The sugarcane was densely packed and almost ten feet tall. The plants were nearly mature with thick stalks surrounded by dry brown leaves and topped by plumes of greenery. A brisk wind rustled through the field.

By the time I arrived, Mac, our platoon sergeant, had already devised a plan. The easiest way to flush out the Japanese would've been to burn the field. But Mac knew the farmers in the area. They were desperately poor, and the cane was their only source of income. Talking it over with the men, Mac decided to forego the burning and make a pass through the field on foot. I went along with the plan, and was glad I didn't have to make the decision.

Six of us got in a skirmish line spaced about five yards apart. We started through the field while the four others waited to fire on any Japanese who ran out. We crept forward with our rifles at the ready. The dry rustling from the wind covered the noise of our approach. Our only visibility was occasionally between the rows. Otherwise, you couldn't see much more than a few feet in front of you.

I glanced through a small opening in the cane, and spotted a Japanese soldier sitting on the ground. I looked at the back of his cloth cap. He was facing away from me. The range was thirty feet. I aimed my rifle at the center of his back and fired. He slumped forward, shot through the heart. Without changing position, I shot him twice more in the back of the head. It was a way to release some tension. I quickly reloaded before approaching the body.

By this time, I'd seen a lot of dead soldiers and many kinds of wounds. But I wasn't prepared for what I saw next.

He was still sitting hunched over and had blood on the back of his head. I reached across with my right hand, grabbed his left shoulder, and pulled him on to his back. I recoiled inwardly as the bright sun reflected off what had been a human face. There were no teeth, no nose, no eyes, nothing from the bottom of his chin to the top of his forehead and between his ears except an uneven pink and white cone-shaped gash that narrowed to two small holes in the back of his skull. There was almost no blood. I had used two 150 grain steel-jacketed .30 caliber bullets that traveled at 2,700 feet per second. This was the result from thirty feet.

I felt the eyes of Filipino locals upon me. They were courteously waiting for me to finish frisking the enemy for souvenirs and intelligence so that they could grab his clothes and boots. I tried to play it cool and not betray my shock at the blown-out face. A shout from the edge of the cane field gave me an out.

Mac had shot another enemy soldier in the field, which meant there should have been one more left. But the guys manning the perimeter said that eight Japanese had run out of the sugarcane after hearing our shots. They'd scampered across an open field and into another stand of rustling cane. This time, two of our men went to the upwind end of the field and set it on fire while the rest of us waited downwind with rifles raised.

Six Japanese emerged and tried to shoot at us,

but we cut them down. The other two committed suicide with satchel charges. A large group of Filipino farmers who had been watching the operation cheered. We returned to our outpost with no casualties.

****

Our company of 220 men that had made the beachhead on January 9 was now down to around seventy. About fifteen of these casualties were killed in action and perhaps sixty more wounded in combat. The rest were due to sickness, disease, and battle fatigue.

Heavy combat is chaotic, and it's hard to keep track of everyone in your platoon, even if you're a leader. Sometimes, people would go missing, and until I talked with a medic, maybe even weeks later, I didn't know if they'd been killed, wounded, or evacuated. The non-battle casualties were especially difficult to notice. We lost several men to blood poisoning. Everyone tried to keep their open sores covered, but we were always sweaty and brushing against foliage, and flies were everywhere. Besides, the white of the bandage attracted enemy eyes, so sometimes it was safer to remove it and take our chances.

Hepatitis, yellow jaundice, malaria, and dengue fever were other diseases that caused attrition in our ranks. Only serious cases got evacuated. As one medic had said in an early New Guinea campaign, "If we'd taken everyone off the line who had a fever of 101 or over, we wouldn't have anyone left."

Battle fatigue claimed a share of men, but not nearly as many as disease. The first symptoms were the eyes, the "thousand yard stare," sometimes followed by crying or shaking. The 169th Regiment in the New Georgia campaign had a great number of cases. By one count, almost a quarter of the regiment had to be removed from combat for at least twenty-four hours due to it. On Luzon, there was much less battle fatigue. Our 103d Regiment had just a handful of guys who couldn't hack battle. They'd break down and then get sent to the rear. Many returned and performed well.

Sometimes cowards would feign shaking and crying to avoid duty. It wasn't a common practice probably because the easier out was to stop taking atabrine, our anti-malarial tablets. Malaria was ubiquitous on Luzon, and without atabrine a soldier would come down with chills and a fever in a short time. I'm impressed that so few took this route. Perhaps it helped that us noncoms made sure our men took the bitter-tasting yellow pill every day and learned to recognize the jaundiced hue atabrine gave our faces.

I know of only one self-inflicted gunshot wound during combat. He was a replacement sergeant like me. The medics took one look at his foot and refused to treat it. They made him bandage the wound himself.

In our debilitated state, L Company, along with the rest of our 3d battalion, was assigned "mopping up" duties along a ridge system that stretched east from Hill 355 to south of Mount Alava, a squat cinder-cone volcano prominent enough to receive a name rather than just a number. Elements of two Japanese infantry battalions remained stubbornly entrenched among these hills, despite several attacks by our 169th Regiment. Our job was to finish them off.

We manned a defensive perimeter near the top of Mount Alava. Our battalion's I Company was preparing to attack the enemy about a mile away using five tanks. We had a clear view of the action from our mountaintop perch. We were shot-up, worn-out, and badly in need of rest, but were still better off than I Company, which had suffered the kamikaze attack at sea and were now down to forty or so men. That they were being ordered to make another attack was almost inconceivable.

I watched the spectacle in silent dismay through a binocular borrowed from an officer. Olive-drab figures rose from their foxholes and advanced uphill in crouching positions against enemy fire. I could tell, from almost a mile away, that none of these men wanted to do it, and I mentally bled for them.

Two enemy shells exploded. The smoke and dust cleared to reveal motionless bodies scattered on the hillside. One of the five tanks was hit and burst into flames. The attack bogged down before it even started.

Frank Fecser, one of the seven or eight men left in my squad, came up to me as I stared through the binocular.

"You know, this sounds crazy," said Frank in a hushed voice, "but I kind of wish I was over there with 'em."

I had been thinking the very same thing.

While we were dug in on Mount Alava, our company's acting commander, Lieutenant Foell, called me to his post.

"Gruenfeld, how would you like to become an officer?" he asked.

Foell, like everyone else, thought I was twenty-two years old, but I remained acutely aware that, in fact, I was too young to vote. It seemed a bit premature for me to become an officer. Unlike the veterans who had shipped overseas in November 1942, I was still considered a replacement soldier, and replacements rarely got commissioned so quickly. Also, I was only Staff Sergeant and squad leader, not a First Sergeant and platoon leader like Mac.

"Sir, honestly, I don't know," I replied. "I haven't thought about it, and I like my squad a lot."

"Well, think it over, Jay," he said warmly. "You don't have to decide now."

I returned to our squad and told some of my men about it. Most of them urged me to take the commission. "Think how proud your mom and dad would be," offered Fecser.

I did consider their pride and my own, for I regarded a battlefield commission to be a high honor. Most Army commissions are awarded upon graduation from officer candidate school (OCS), a military academy, or a college ROTC program. We called newly-minted OCS officers "Ninety Day Wonders" in cutting reference to their ninety days of training and lack of real combat experience. Battlefield commissions were earned the hard way, and they came largely by virtue of proven leadership in the field.

Of course, there was always the possibility that I wouldn't survive long enough to accept a commission, even if it were offered. Our company received orders to move on to a nearby hill mass and prepare for a morning attack in the manner of I Company's failed operation. We occupied a series of deep World War I-style trenches that had been dug and abandoned by the Japanese. A couple of blown-up tanks marked the location. The trenches were elaborately camouflaged with sweet potato vines and were virtually undetectable unless you were right on top of them. We shared a trench with the other remaining squad led by a sergeant named Jameson.

I'd bunked with Jameson for a while on New Zealand. He was a veteran of the New Guinea campaign, a 43d Division original, and I didn't think much of him. He milked minor wounds and ailments as long as he could and then returned as slowly as possible back to the line. On the night before our scheduled attack, I met with him and a few others in the trench to go over some details.

As dusk settled over our vine roof, Jameson began complaining loudly about our battle orders.

"I think we should refuse to make the attack," he argued. "We should just say no. Did you see what happened to I Company? They got destroyed! We're too tired. We're too weak. We don't have enough men. We'll get killed."

He groused on and on in this manner, well in the earshot of his squad and most of mine too. I kept quiet, expecting our platoon guide, a good soldier named Dumain, to put a halt to this demoralizing diatribe. When it became clear that

Dumain wasn't going to interject, I raised my voice.

"You can't fight a war like that. You can't just say no," I countered. "I know we're tired. Everyone's tired. But we'll do ok. I don't think it's going to be so bad."

"How can you say it won't be bad?" Jameson responded, unwilling to let the matter die. "The Japs still have plenty of artillery, and they'll use it on us. We need reinforcements to make an attack like this!"

"If they say attack in the morning, then we'll attack in the morning. My squad will make this attack!" I replied emphatically so that all my men could hear. Then, I turned and walked away to the opposite side of the trench.

Later that night, we received a message from battalion headquarters. The morning attack was cancelled.

****

I spent my final days in L Company on cave patrols atop Hill 355. The Japanese had been all but eliminated. Those still surviving were holed up in a series of caves that had been dug into the side of the hill along a well used trail. There were no roads in this area. A company headquarters officer instructed me and my assistant squad leader

Ashey to investigate these hideouts. We were to take six hours and return well before dusk.

"Get a prisoner if you can," the officer ordered, "but don't take any chances to do it."

I was given fifteen soldiers for the mission, including the remaining members of my squad. Before leaving the company area, I told the men our objectives and again emphasized the need for silence. Getting their attention wasn't difficult. They were now all experienced combat infantry. Our only problem was that we were green on cave work.

I knew that hand grenades would be our primary tools. They were the infantry's in-house artillery and usually came in three different types. The fragmentation grenade was the most common. It weighed twenty ounces, had a 4.6 second fuse, and burst into fragments when the TNT inside exploded. The white phosphorus grenade produced concussion, white smoke and burning bits of phosphorus that couldn't be doused with water. The third kind were various colors of smoke grenades that we used for concealment and signaling.

No one taught us how to do this work. We learned on the job, using our experiences with pillboxes to guide the sequence of our approach. We figured we'd usually start by throwing in a white phosphorous grenade, followed by a fragmentation grenade. The smoke and fire of the white phosphorous would make it difficult for the enemy to find the second grenade and throw it back.

We made our way along the trail, past isolated tree stands and above brushy draws. We came to the first cave. I put out-guards on each side of us so we wouldn't be surprised by enemy patrols and then got to work. One of my men reported hearing a voice in the cave, so I knew it was occupied. I wanted to avoid a head-on approach, so I crawled toward the left side of the cave's mouth to accommodate my right-handed throw. When I got within eight or ten feet of the opening, I pulled the pin on the grey cylinder with a white "WP" stenciled on it. I held the grenade for two seconds and then threw it in. I didn't want to give the enemy time to toss it back. A flash of white phosphorus, then a loud roar, then smoke billowing from the cave entrance. We followed up with two fragmentation grenades, which also exploded, and waited for the dust to settle. It was deathly quiet.

I got up and cautiously moved toward the cavity, which was surprisingly little, about six-by-ten feet. Crouching low, I fired into the corners.

There were two bodies, one especially small. I grabbed the small man's heel and pulled him clear out of the cave with one tug. He rolled downhill a few yards and came to a stop. My men searched him for souvenirs and intelligence.

The second body was heavier. As I dragged him out, I noticed the brains from his shattered skulls trailing six or seven feet behind him on the dusty cave floor and entrance. Since I was now a combat veteran experienced at hiding true feelings, I feigned nonchalance and acted as if this were a routine happening.

After the initial grenading on the third cave, I spotted the legs of a Japanese soldier just inside on the left. I shot his legs at least four times before entering. There was another enemy on the right, but I could see he was dead, so I turned to look at the man I'd shot on the left. He was reaching for his rifle despite his wounds. My bayonet was a few inches from his throat, but I just couldn't plunge it in. I shot him instead, and my ears rang for a couple of days afterward. Bayoneting would have been hard on him and me both.

It took us about an hour to do the first half-dozen caves. I did most of the grenading and all the first throws. On the seventh cave, a tall lanky soldier, not from my squad, stepped up and asked if he could toss the first grenade. I quickly agreed and coached him a little, cautioning him especially to hold the grenade a couple seconds before throwing it. The lanky soldier nodded in agreement but apparently with little understanding.

Gripping a fragmentation grenade, the soldier walked straight up to the opening, pulled the pin and, without waiting an instant, hurled the metal canister as hard as he could.

The grenade ricocheted off the interior cave walls and then bounced back out and landed at the soldier's feet. He had two or three seconds to find cover.

It says much about our squad's exhausted state that we laughed uproariously at the sight of this lanky soldier trying to save himself. If we'd been in civilian life or Basic Training, we'd have chewed him out and then offered further instruction. Instead, we doubled over in laughter and didn't stop even after the grenade exploded and the lanky soldier emerged shaken but in one piece. He didn't offer to throw any more grenades.

After the final cave, we turned back up the trail toward our company headquarters. As we approached the defense perimeter, I spotted the gloomy faces of Lieutenant Foell and another officer who looked as if they were expecting bad news from us. After a lot of firing and a couple dozen grenades exploding, Foell probably worried we'd suffered some casualties.

"We're all here!" I shouted cheerfully.

We claimed twelve dead enemy, some useful looking Japanese papers and a map, and a pile of souvenirs to add to our collections.

****

On February 13, 1945, the Army declared the Lingayen Gulf beachhead secure and ordered the 43d Division put into reserve to rest, re-quip, and replace the men we'd lost. Our undermanned and beat-up company began a long march back from those numbered hills to the town of Santa Barbara, about five miles from where we'd landed on January 9th. I was exhausted, more so than usual, and really dragged myself back to the rest camp. Along the way, we saw members of the 33d Infantry Division who had just landed and were moving inland to take up our old positions. A rather grim joke passed through our ranks about one of these 33d Division guys asking us a question on the road:

"What platoon are you?" inquires the fresh soldier.

"Platoon, hell! We're L Company!" we respond.

The tent camp with its showers, cots, clean clothes and hot meals seemed like heaven. Until then, our only bath had been one short dip in a river with out-guards posted. Our meals had been mostly K rations, which were designed only to be eaten for a few days at a time. Canned meat or cheese and crackers provided the main sustenance with sugar, cigarettes, chewing gum, a candy bar, and powdered coffee as sides. The introduction of the heartier and more variable C rations helped to break the monotony of our meals.

After thirty-five days of catching just a couple hours sleep at a time on the ground, we most looked forward to lying in a nice dry cot. I collapsed in mine the first night and expected to fall asleep instantly, like I always did in the field. Instead, I tossed and turned. The canvas cot felt confining. So, I took my pillow and blanket and laid them on the ground. That did the trick. When I woke the next morning, I looked around the tent. Three others out of a dozen were on the ground too.

On February 15, two days after being taken off the line, our platoon's first sergeant marched into my tent.

"Gruenfeld," he ordered, "go down to Regimental headquarters and get sworn in."

"For what?" I asked.

"To be an officer," he replied flatly.

Four of us in the regiment received commissions that day. The ceremony took all of ten minutes, including time to pin on my gold bars, which were donated by a lieutenant, Don Shaw, who had come to us from the 41st Division. As I left the building

and passed a Filipino guard, he presented arms—
my first salute. I later learned that, according to
custom, I should have given him a silver dollar.

Four days later, Loren McAllister received his
commission. I joked that I was now his senior,
since I'd been commissioned before him. He responded that talk of seniority among second lieutenants is like speaking of virtue in a whorehouse.

The most distressing part of my becoming an
officer was leaving L Company. The Army rightly
figured that newly commissioned officers might
have trouble commanding the proper respect of
their old buddies, so the policy was to reassign 2d
lieutenants to another part of the regiment. The
great Audie Murphy rebuffed countless offers of
commissions simply because he didn't want to
leave his men. The Army eventually issued Murphy a special waiver that allowed him to stay with
his company.

In my case, it soon became clear that Regimental
headquarters wanted to give me a heavy weapons platoon. I didn't know mortars and machine guns very
well and protested that I belonged with riflemen.

"Weapons is a safer assignment, Jay," explained
my new battalion's personnel officer. "You won't
be so far up front."

It was true that rifle platoon leaders had the
shortest life span in the Army, but I wanted to be

up front because that's what I knew. Someone took my case to Lieutenant Colonel Lloyd Barron, a battalion commander. Barron listened and gave me the last available rifle platoon: 2d Platoon, C Company, 1st Battalion.

I marked the occasion with a letter to my parents:

Feb. 18, 1945
Dear Dad,
   Please send some food, like sardines, crackers, etc.
   This is just a short letter to you. As you can see by the return address, it is Lieutenant Jay now. I was given a direct appointment without going to O.C.S. I guess it is a little more of an honor that way. Now the responsibility is greater. I often led my squad by being at its head, but you can't control a platoon when you are lead man so that will be one difference. Just wish you were here so I could hear yours and Mother's advice and encouragement. We did a good job, Dad, and are damn proud of our outfit.
   Went to church this morning for the first time since leaving the ship, and really enjoyed it a lot.
   Lots of love,
   Jay

****

Platoons vary in quality. I inherited a fine one whose virtues became apparent to me soon after walking into C Company's tent camp and shaking hands with my new comrades. The company hadn't been decimated in the Solomon Island campaigns, so it retained a large number of experienced noncoms. It wasn't unusual to have a twenty-two-year-old sergeant who'd been in the Army four years, overseas twenty-seven months, and seasoned by two campaigns before Luzon. The medic who had long served with the 2d platoon told me that he hadn't treated a single case of battle fatigue in the platoon (and never did). The news cheered me, though I raised an eyebrow at the man who delivered it.

By all counts, Harry Horne was a superior combat medic, though "a little different." A true eccentric from Johnstown, Pennsylvania, Harry was anything but general issue. When I met him, he was wearing shorts, aviator sunglasses, and a green Australian army officer's shirt complete with epaulets. He followed his own regulations and somehow managed to stay almost perfectly clean no matter how grungy the rest of us got.

I arrived at the same time as about fifteen fresh replacements, an infusion of troops that brought our 2d platoon up to full fighting strength. These

new guys all had names beginning with "B." They
had been assigned alphabetically, Army style.

Right away, I convened the forty men for an
orientation meeting in a tent. I emphasized the
cerebral element of combat, the importance of being aware of your surroundings and keeping an
eye out for things that don't look quite right, like
a brush pile in a dry creek bed.

"And for God's sake, count your shots when you
fire," I warned. "You should always know how many
rounds you have left in your rifle. You never want
to pull that trigger and have nothing happen."

I told the veterans to mentor the new guys so
that they don't make any deadly mistakes.

"Don't tell them any bullshit," I said. "Teach
them what you've learned."

The vets did most of the talking from there on
in. At one point, I off-handedly mentioned an incident I witnessed where a soldier from another
platoon had run from his position on Hill 600 instead standing fast in the face of enemy fire.

From the middle of the pack of men, a blonde-
haired replacement, only six months in the Army,
piped up.

"Why that yellow son-of-a-bitch."

Mighty tough talk coming from someone who'd
never seen combat. But I liked his aggressive attitude, and I made a point to keep an eye on him.

His name was Virgil Brumfield, a twenty-two-year-old father of three from Huntington, West Virginia.

Unbeknownst to me at the time, I came to the new platoon with something of a reputation. Combat medics had their own grapevine, and Harry Horne had passed word that I was a "Jap killer" who had zapped more enemy than anyone in L Company. I bolstered my rep by accident one day when ten of us went on a chicken hunt. Chickens were everywhere on Luzon since many Filipinos had abandoned their farms during the Japanese occupation.

A brightly colored rooster flew across a little creek and lit in a tree about forty yards away. I told the guys I would take it. Since I was shooting high powered .30 caliber bullets, I knew to be careful where I aimed. I didn't want to end up with mostly feathers and skin.

I put on my rifle sling and sat down to shoot. My rifle was zeroed almost perfectly, and I'd memorized its ballistics, so I knew where it would hit at any range if I shot correctly. To save meat I held very high on the rooster's shoulder, maybe an inch and a half below its head since he was crouched a little.

I pulled the trigger, and he fell straight down, beating his wings rapidly.

"Great shot, Jay!" cheered the guys.

When they went to retrieve the bird, they found that the bullet had clipped the rooster's head clean off. I didn't tell them that I had shot a little high.

A few minutes later, a hen ran across the creek and up a little hill. The men fired eight to ten shots, but it kept going. For them, it was a pretty tough shot since the bird was crossing in front at a dead run. For me, on the other hand, the shot was a fairly easy one since the hen was running straight away in the opposite direction, almost as if it were standing still. I pulled the trigger offhand (standing) and made a clean kill that saved practically all the meat. My reputation as a super-shot was established. A couple weeks later, after cave patrol where a group of us fired on three enemy soldiers, killing all three, I heard a replacement say, "Yeah, Jay got two and we got the third one." There was no way to tell who actually scored, but because of my rep, I got the credit.

****

At daybreak on February 24, the fourth anniversary of the 43d Division's activation, I clambered aboard a deuce-and-a-half truck for a ride to San Fabian Cemetery. Most officers complained about having to attend the division's memorial service and passed it off on the new guys like me. I was not only willing but eager to witness that most moving ceremony.

We drove through the early morning countryside, and for the first time I noted the pastoral scenery of the island. We passed young boys asleep on the backs of the huge carabao they were herding. I arrived at the cemetery in a reflective mood.

Over 600 perfectly aligned white wooden crosses marked the resting places of the men from our division killed in action since January 9. We assembled on the east side of the cemetery. An honor guard with rifles stood across from us. Palm trees swayed in the morning breeze. General Walter Krueger, commander of the entire Sixth Army, took the podium and paid tribute to the honored dead and to us, the living, their comrades.

"No division has done more than the 43d in this campaign," he intoned.

He may have said that to the ten other divisions who participated in the invasion, but I took a measure of pride in Krueger's approval.

My men and I received another important affirmation shortly before we moved back into combat. I'd been gathering some replacements for occasional details that involved scrounging building materials to make frames for our mosquito nets. These often took us to the well-provisioned Clark Field, the Luzon air base overrun by the Japanese in January 1942 and recently taken back by American ground forces after heavy fighting. We got to know some of the Air Corps guys, soldiers we normally didn't have much contact with.

Infantrymen had a love/hate relationship with the Air Corps. On the one hand, we appreciated and relied upon their support in combat operations (except when they dropped their bombs on us). On the other hand, we were jealous of them. Back home, they were the glamour boys, the stars of the war. Most kids grew up wanting to be pilots. And why wouldn't they? Air Corps guys got better pay, better food, better sleeping quarters, more medals, and faster promotions than ground forces men.

That's what made it especially gratifying in the final days of our rest when some crewmen at Clark Field treated us—a bunch of ragtag infantry guys—to lunch in their rather well-appointed mess. We sat at tables draped in white tablecloths with folded napkins. And, topping it off, the servers were the airmen themselves who said how indebted they were to us for the hard lives we led and the price we paid for liberating their air base. I felt proud to wear the Combat Infantry Badge, and that lunch remains one of my finest memories of the war.

****

We moved back to the frontlines in early March. Battalion headquarters informed me that 2d platoon would soon be reinforced to make a major patrol, my first with the new outfit.

I knew that my future as the leader of these forty veterans and green-as-grass replacements would depend on how I performed on this assignment. I think they considered their performance also, though the replacements probably thought most about surviving. The focus of my thoughts and prayers was on fulfilling the mission with a minimum of casualties.

A battalion intelligence officer gave me a map and explained what we were to do. The enemy held the high ground, as usual. Their defensive positions were part of the Shimbu Line, which stretched across thirty-five miles of formidable mountain terrain east of Manila. Forty thousand Japanese had withdrawn from the capital city and toted artillery, mortars, vehicles, and plenty of ammunition and rations into the volcanic cave-pocked hills surrounding it. Manila would never be secure until we dislodged the enemy from their mountain fortress.

My platoon, supplemented by a 60mm mortar squad of five men, was to start at daylight and reconnoiter to the south a couple miles, then turn east and try to cross a range of steep hills. Once across, we'd run into a blacktop road controlled by American forces. If all went well, we'd be riding back to our base in trucks that night.

The intelligence officer told me to expect enemy contact and take note of the strength of any positions we encountered. The orders sounded familiar, but a little spooky, especially since we would cover a lot of distance and return after dark. The starting point was just south of the town of Antipolo, which, in turn, was twelve miles dead east of Manila. We would head down the Morong Peninsula, a mountainous finger of land sticking deep into Laguna de Bay, a huge fresh water lake. The main terrain feature was Bench Mark 7, a high rocky hill held by the enemy. The Japanese fired big noisy rockets off of Bench Mark 7, and one of our jobs was to pinpoint the launch site.

The morning broke hot and humid, but clear. As we prepared to move out, a squad leader came to me saying that Virgil Brumfield wanted to serve as a scout. Brum had been trained in antiaircraft artillery but had been thrown into the infantry because of the need for men. Now, he and his buddy Joe Briones, another replacement, were requesting positions that would put them in closest contact with the enemy. There normally wasn't much competition for scouting jobs.

Benchmark 7, the launching site of Japanese rockets, which we pinpointed on my first patrol with the 2nd platoon in March 1945. (*U.S. Army, Department of Defense*)

"Ok if the new guys serve as scouts?" the sergeant asked.

"We might as well see what they can do," I replied.

Brum and Briones set out in front of our loose single file squad column. The terrain was open, and after about a half-mile, we began to receive some long-range rifle fire.

The sound lessons I'd been accumulating since Basic Training kicked in. Crack...pop. Crack... pop. There was a nice gap between the crack of the bullet overhead and the fainter pop of the rifle discharging at its source. These shots were coming from 600 yards away or more, and the veterans in the platoon just kept walking as if they didn't even hear the fire. "Just another day at the office," as one of my sergeants put it. The replacements, however, darted their eyes nervously.

After six or seven rounds, Brum turned back to me.

"What is that?"

"That's a Jap sniper firing at us," I casually explained to him.

"Where is he? I'll go get him," he said with dogged determination.

I liked the fearless response, even if it betrayed naïveté.

After an hour, the sniper fire stopped, and the hike took on a rather pleasant and leisurely aspect. With no need for silence, Harry Horne began quoting snatches of Kipling as we walked behind the lead squad. I quoted some back, mostly from *Gunga Din* and *The Young British Soldier*, which clearly delighted the literary-minded medic.

When yer officer's dead and yer sergeant looks white,
Remember it's ruin to run from a fight.
Just take open order, lay down and sit tight,
And wait for supports like a soldier,
A soldier of the Queen.

We passed three local men and one woman gathering cashews nuts and fruit. As a forester, I was curious about the trees. I'd never seen one before. I ordered the platoon to halt for a break. We put out-guards and watched the bucolic harvest scene. The cashew fruit or "apple," it turns out, is sweet and edible, and what we call the nut hangs off the end.

We lit out again on our trek over gently rolling hills with few trails and no roads. As we approached a wide-open grassy area with a patch of trees on the other side, I got an ominous feeling. This was a place to be careful. We stopped about 300 yards from the opposite timber line. After talking with the veteran platoon sergeant, Johnny Herrick, and the veteran platoon guide, Larry Daley, both from Maine, they agreed that Brum and I would scout the area before having the others cross the opening. The men would provide fire support in case we ran into trouble.

Brum and I started out in leap-frog fashion. Brum covered me while I ran ahead ten or twenty yards and hit the ground behind one of the low grassy mounds scattered across the area. Then, Brum took his turn running, passing me up while I lay prone with my rifle ready.

We did this several times. It grew hot and quiet. As Brum approached the tree line on the other side of the open field, the hair on the back of my neck stood on end. Brum flopped down, brought his rifle to his shoulder, and fired about thirty yards into the trees. Lying behind him, I immediately squeezed off eight rounds and reloaded, while our platoon, observing the action, opened up with a wall of fire. I yelled to Brum to withdraw, and after he passed I followed him back to the platoon, which was still laying down heavy fire.

I swelled with confidence in my new outfit. They'd just proven that they weren't reluctant to fire their weapons, a frequent problem with green platoons.

A brief strategy meeting with Herrick, Daley, and the squad leaders yielded a consensus on how to proceed. We'd probe the enemy position but avoid a prolonged firefight if we could. Once we had a good feel for what they had and where they were, we'd pull back on my voice signal or on Herrick's in the event I was put out of action.

Most of the platoon would provide a base of fire from the left flank while I would accompany a squad led by Sergeant Harlow to make the attack. Harlow was reputed to have killed more Japanese than anyone in the battalion.

Herrick, my second in command, insisted on joining the attack party. Our squad moved across the opening in a solid wave with five yards between each man. I was on the extreme left, visible to those giving supporting fire. The man to my right stayed slightly behind me, and the man to his right stayed slightly behind him, and so forth down the line. We shot into the trees as we advanced.

From our left, riflemen kept up heavy and accurate support fire, while the mortar squad lobbed ten rounds right into the tree line. Soon we were within a few yards of the enemy position and firing hard to keep them pinned down.

Suddenly, out of the corner of my eye to my left, I spotted something rise up out of a foxhole. It was a Japanese soldier about twenty feet away. I immediately jerked around and fired without aiming in order to buy some time to line up a good shot. Then, I aimed quickly and pulled the trigger.

Nothing. My rifle was empty. I hadn't counted my shots. I hit the ground and so did the enemy soldier who began receiving fire from others in my squad. Lying on my back, I reloaded my rifle and then unclipped a grenade from my shirt pocket. I pulled the pin, let the handle go, counted to two, and then tried delicately to toss the grenade into the enemy foxhole.

"Oh shit, it's short!" I thought.

The grenade hit the ground in front of the foxhole and slowly rolled straight, dropping into the hole like a perfectly putted golf ball into a cup.

The air in front of me exploded with flesh and torn equipment. I clearly saw a pack strap fly through the air. I heard cheers from my right and looked over to see the whole squad firing, diving for cover, and throwing grenades.

Harlow had a Japanese soldier lined up in his sights right in front of him at thirty feet. The enemy had his arm cocked, ready to hurl a grenade. Harlow squeezed the trigger, but his rifle jammed, so he ducked behind a log where Herrick happened to be. Two Japanese grenades followed him and exploded at the same time. I expected the worst.

A few minutes later, a voice called out from the rear. It was our medic Harry Horne.

"Cover me!" he shouted, as he ran across open ground to Harlow and Herrick's position.

Bright sunlight reflected off the medical pouches and equipment that Harry quickly arrayed around the men. It was inspiring to see him work, even more so when he called out "Cover me!" again and rose with his arm around Harlow's waist, and Harlow's arm around Harry's neck. Herrick limped behind them, making it out under his own power.

"Pull back!" I shouted to the squad. I stayed behind firing while the men withdrew in twos and threes. I was about to follow when Harlow and Herrick cried that they had left their rifles behind the log.

"Would you get them, Jay?"

I thought twice about running over to grab them. But the platoon was laying down such heavy fire, and I wanted to impress the troops. I dashed over to the log, picked up the rifles, and ran crouching back to our lines, burdened by the twenty extra pounds. Exhilarated and relieved, I got near our fire base and blurted, "Rifles for sale! Rifles for sale!" The guys laughed.

We radioed back to battalion headquarters and reported what had happened. I asked battalion if they wanted us to take the enemy position or continue our mission. They replied, "Continue the mission," and we all breathed easier.

We still had a long way to go, and our numbers were down. We left the two wounded with litter bearers and a few riflemen. Battalion would send out a patrol to assist their return.

We headed east, away from the enemy foxholes and into steep jungle terrain that looked ideal for defensive positions. As we reached the crest of a hill, we spotted a couple Japanese soldiers running into dense foliage. I halted the platoon and turned to Larry Daley, who, with Herrick gone, was now second in command.

Though a veteran, Daley had seen little combat because he had been wounded shortly after making the beachhead in January. Despite mortar fragments in his stomach, Daley hadn't wanted to leave the line, so he asked Harry Horne, who was treating him, to fish three or four inches in and find the metal shards. Horne tried and failed, so Daley was sent to the rear. He'd only recently gotten out of the hospital, and this was his first day back in action.

Daley agreed to scout the area with me while the rest of the platoon stayed behind. We waded through knee-high grass and began drawing enough rifle fire from 200 yards that we hit the ground and started to crawl. Like in the rice paddy with Mac, it was sticky hot, and the crawling became intolerable.

"Why don't we make a run for it?" asked Daley.

"Ok," I said, "who should go first?"

"You," he offered gallantly.

I jolted upright and ran as fast as I could uphill. Shots followed me, but nothing close. I reached cover and hit the ground.

The Japanese now knew that Daley would be next, and they were ready for him. He ran up the hill with enemy fire cracking all around him. Somehow, he made it to my position and flopped down pulling at his equipment. I noticed a pack strap dangling, severed by a bullet.

"Are you ok?" I asked.

"Yeah, but look at this," he huffed, opening his

shirt front to reveal a red stripe across his chest that looked like it had been drawn with lipstick. A bullet had also gone through his shirt pocket, cutting his pipe in two.

We adjusted our course and sent Brum and Briones out in front just south of where the enemy shots had originated. It was well past noon, and we were two miles away from the blacktop road that marked the end of our patrol. We drew no further fire, even as we neared the Japanese position, and figured that they had withdrawn.

We hiked steadily uphill into thick jungle broken by expanses of jagged rock. Broken blisters pocked the rock surface, and the edges were sharp enough to cut through our boot leather. We grew tired as we wrestled with vines and brush just to keep moving forward.

I jumped ahead to the front of the platoon, just behind the scouts and the lead squad leader. Briones came back to me, clearly distressed, almost in tears.

"Look what happened," he said sheepishly, holding part of his rifle in one hand and part in the other.

A vine had caught in the trigger guard and pulled the trigger group out. The trigger group was gone, and so he couldn't put the rifle back together. I told him fix bayonet and have Harry Horne tape up the rifle.

"You'd better pray we don't get into another fire-fight," I said with a scowl, which was half-faked.

We reached the crest of the short mountain and took a break to recover from our arduous climb. Soon as we started back up, Brum report hearing voices.

"Nuts!" I thought. "Here we go again."

Brum and I crept forward and listened carefully. A dog barked and voices began shouting at each other in Japanese.

We were about a half-mile from the blacktop road. We decided to turn a little south and continue on, trying to remain especially quiet.

We made it to the road, and one of the battalion's scout cars soon drove up. A soldier got out and told us to march to a nearby junction where a truck was waiting.

We arrived at the junction as darkness fell. After we ate some rations, a lieutenant oriented us on our journey back to camp.

"Remember," he said emphatically and repeatedly, "the first six bridges you'll come to are blown up. It's dark and you have to be careful. Six blown bridges. You're gonna have to leave the road and ford a creek or cross a dry bed six times to get back."

Somehow we loaded our entire platoon and equipment on to one two-and-a-half ton truck. Riflemen rode the fenders, peering into an inky dark broken only by the dim yellow rays coming through the little slits of our truck's blackout headlights. We rolled down the rough country rode and carefully navigated the creek crossings.

After the sixth bridge, we sped up a bit until we came to the seventh. The driver started confidently across until the men on the fenders began frantically waving their arms and shouting for us to stop.

I got out, walked a few feet ahead, and stared straight down about fifty feet into a dry creek bed. Seven bridges had been blown, not six.

We reached camp after midnight and staggered off to find a place to sleep. I should have ordered the men to dig foxholes. But another unit had sentries out, there was no action, and we were so exhausted, we just flopped down on some level ground and fell asleep. That night we got some incoming artillery, but most of us slept right through it.

Before losing consciousness, I reflected on the day. I couldn't imagine a better first patrol. The 2d platoon was obviously a honey. We were rested, replenished, and proud. If an artillery round had dropped on me that night, I would have died happy.

A few days later, based on the information we'd gathered, our entire company of 200 headed for the Japanese position we'd first encountered on our patrol. We got there to find that the enemy had pulled out. The infantryman I'd killed with the grenade had been buried in his foxhole. His comrades had left on his grave a hand-sized silver saber wrapped in cloth. The men muttered "nice touch" in acknowledgment, then grabbed the saber as a souvenir.

Our company dug in for the night after forming a perimeter just north of the vacated enemy position. Shortly before dawn, an enemy unit walked right into our lines at the opposite end of the perimeter from where my platoon was sleeping. The Japanese were practically to our company's foxholes when our men opened fire. It was a massacre. At first light, we scoped the area, and I saw at least thirty enemy bodies scattered about. We'd suffered not a single casualty. I picked up a Japanese saber.

"I wish the Japs had come into our side of the perimeter," complained a couple of my guys.

I smiled and nodded in approval.

CHAPTER SIX

The Fighting Deuce

March-May 1945

The 103d Regiment's successful attack on Benchmark 7 helped to dislodge the Japanese from its southern anchor on the Shimbu Line. The enemy withdrew six miles east to well-prepared mountain defenses that stretched north to south across two river valleys. We followed on their heels and fought them on volcanic rises bearing such names as Mt. Quitago, Mt. Balidbiran, and Benchmark 21.

After arriving at an outpost among these ridges in mid-March, we received a hand-carried load of grenades for cave patrols. "Be careful with these," warned the supply party leader, "they have new shorter fuses." We'd heard this several times before, and I'd never found it to be true. Just in case, I grabbed two grenades, walked to the edge of our perimeter, and tested them. They exploded in about 4.6 seconds, just like they were supposed to. From then on, I told my guys to operate under the assumption that the fuses were correct. But the rumors didn't die, and I'm sure they caused premature throws across the Pacific.

I instructed the replacements in the art of blowing up caves. Everyone had to carry at least three grenades and be prepared to borrow from others. One had to be careful when taking someone else's grenades because each soldier set the pins differently. Hand grenades had cotter pins that went through the handle. Like hairpins, they were bent pieces of soft metal with two tines at one end and a large finger ring on the other. Some guys feared the pins falling out, so they splayed the tines back. The problem with this precaution came in combat when soldiers had trouble pulling the splayed pins, something that happened to me once or twice. When action was imminent, I kept my pins pretty straight and at the ready, but I borrowed some bent ones too.

On my first cave patrol with the 2d platoon, a replacement partnered with me. He crouched behind while I pulled the pin and held the grenade with my arm cocked for two full seconds. After

In January 1995, on the 50th anniversary of the Lingayen Gulf invasion, I returned to the site of my first patrol and took this photograph. The platoon crossed the skyline near the centerline of the photo and then hiked east (right to left). (*Author's collection*)

letting it fly, I turned my head away and caught a glimpse of my deathly white partner. He'd almost wet his pants staring at that live grenade in his face.

We became cave patrol experts as we blew many of them over the next several weeks. Many of their occupants died when they ran out and we shot them. Others died in their caves. We scored a large number of kills and suffered no casualties, unless you count the grenade fragments in my backside. After seeing the poor job that two Japanese grenades did in their attempt to kill Harlow and Herrick behind the log on my first 2d platoon patrol, I lost respect for that enemy weapon and merely turned my back and bent over when one came rolling in my general direction. The result was some shards of metal, a bandaged rear end, and no Purple Heart. I couldn't rightly accept one for a wound that kept me out of action not even a half-hour.

One of our last cave patrols was a big one. Battalion built it up as a major operation and selected our platoon for the job. The intelligence officer showed me a map of the ridge system. "Go down there and see what you can find in those caves," he said, pointing to a spot on the map below us. "We think there are a lot of Japs in them. Take prisoners if you can," he continued, repeating the now common instruction, "but don't take any chances to do it." Barron, the battalion commander, thought the patrol so important, he watched the whole thing through a binocular from his perch 1,200 yards or so away.

We sneaked up on the first cave, heard someone in there, and I threw a grenade. One kill. We took the same approach with the next cave, which was about a hundred yards away from this first. This time, a Japanese soldier ran out with his hands in the air. I hadn't taken a single prisoner and was happy to see the enemy surrender for once. He seemed to be trying to communicate with us, stammering something that sounded like, "You, you, you, you, you!" Then, one of my squad leaders, Ed Barker, raised his rifle and fired. The Japanese soldier fell backward.

"He had a grenade," explained Ed as we approached the body. Sure enough, a grenade was in his hand, but the grenade hadn't been armed.

We moved on to another cave and killed more Japanese. On about the fourth, we received resistance in the form of those rather ineffectual Japanese fragmentation grenades. One came flying out of the cave entrance and exploded fairly close to me. Not having learned my lesson the first time, I simply turned away instead of hitting the ground. Small pieces of shrapnel sprayed my backside again. There was some blood, but not much.

We reached the final cave, an opening in a sidehill. I followed our standard operating procedure and put two men about fifty yards above and behind the cave to prevent a surprise attack from our rear. One of these was a problem guy, a screw-up who had transferred in from another outfit. Putting him on out-guard kept him out of our way.

I approached the cave entrance from the side and threw a white phosphorus grenade. One Japanese ran out, and we shot him. Then, I threw two grenades. Two ran out, and we shot them. I was preparing to throw three grenades when the cave exploded with machine gun fire. The survivors had set up a light Nambu machine gun to keep us at bay. Chased away from the cave front, we climbed on top of it and carefully began dropping grenades so they exploded at the mouth.

These had the desired effect, and Japanese soldiers began trying to escape, shooting as they came out. We picked them off. Suddenly, fire erupted from the group behind me and came right through our ranks. It was the screw-up out-guard taking shots at the Japanese and almost hitting our guys in the process. I turned and charged screaming up the hill.

"If you take one more downhill shot," I swore, adding a generous dose of expletives, "I promise it will be the last one you ever take!"

We still had the Nambu machine gunner and a few others inside to deal with. It was getting dark, and we were running out of grenades and M1 clips. I ordered the platoon to withdraw, but organized fire on the cave as we pulled back to prevent the enemy from carrying the machine gun out in pursuit.

As we retreated, we heard an explosion inside the cave. A suicide with a grenade. At least those Japanese grenades were good for something, I thought. A few seconds later, another explosion. Suicide number two. Then another, and then another.

We listened to the grisly blasts with glee. After the eighth suicide, one of our guys playfully called, "How about one for the road?" The enemy obliged. A satchel charge, rather than a grenade, claimed the final and ninth victim. The machine gunner kept firing.

I radioed back to our base. "I think our job is done here. I got hit in the tail, and we're coming in." Harry Horne was waiting with methylate and a bandage. This was my third wound, and none of them was medal-worthy. "When you get hit for real, I'm going to stick you with a needle six times just for fun before giving you morphine," he said in mock malice.

We were written up for valor medals for this operation. That we didn't get them was the least of our concerns. The next day, another patrol returned to the final cave with a flamethrower and found nine bodies.

Lieutenant Colonel Barron hailed our performance on this and other missions and put me in for a promotion to 1st lieutenant. Our regimental commander, Colonel Joseph Cleland, turned it down, saying that I'd only been at grade for twenty-eight days. He thought I needed to pay more dues.

Official recognition meant little to me at age

twenty compared to the esteem of my platoon. In combat, one's brothers in arms take precedence over everything. The battlefield is a great equalizer inspiring a down-to-basics standard of judgment. Wealth, status, education, looks—none of it matters. All you care about in separating the good soldier from the bad is whether he will help you survive this trial of fire and get the job done. "Will he be there when I need him? Does he know what he's doing? Does he take his fair share of risks? Is he really trying?" I worked hard to make sure my platoon answered "yes" to these questions when posed about me. That's why I tried to stay near the front of the action, even if the field manuals encouraged platoon leaders to remain further back and direct operations. That's also why I often played the fearless leader, turning my back, rather than hitting the ground, in the face of some Japanese grenades, and shaking off artillery barrages that left me concussed and gasping for air.

Occasionally, I had to censor my platoon's outgoing mail (when no other officer was available for the job), which gave me the opportunity to gather their impressions of me. Replacements especially would sometimes say, "He's not afraid of anything" or "He's always up front," confirming that they appreciated my carrying more than my fair share of the burden, even if it was all an act.

The good reputation of the 2d platoon grew. Joe Briones bragged about "The Fighting Deuce," as he nicknamed us, and others talked of "Gruenfeld's Marauders" and their "commando" style of combat.

One night in a rest area trying to sleep, I heard my least aggressive squad leader talking drunkenly to his assistant.

"I don't know about this commando stuff," the squad leader spat with a hint of derision.

The assistant replied, "As long as I have my little ole rifle, it's ok by me."

That was good to hear.

Soon afterward, a couple of excellent combat noncoms from another platoon approached me in front of my noncoms saying they wanted a transfer to the Fighting Deuce. They had liberated some sake and were feeling good. They talked of taking a reduction in rank to join us. Transferring was impossible, and they knew it, but I was touched and a little proud.

Sometimes my pride got the better of me. When a rival platoon scored just a couple kills with what sounded like 1,000 machine gun rounds, I chastised them.

"Why didn't you just bayonet those Japs instead of wasting all that ammo?" I asked.

I later felt badly for showboating in such a way,

but professional pride in a job well done was important, not least because it helped to displace fear. The determination to do the job right with a minimum of casualties became so powerful that I accepted the accompanying danger.

The lessons learned in battle also helped to assuage our fear. We began to disregard most small arms fire and trusted the protection afforded by rock or folds in the ground or just lying low.

Fear was less a problem in battle than it was in the lulls between fights. Throwing grenades and exchanging fire at close quarters were exhilarating. Often adrenaline surged and pushed aside all worry and concern for safety.

But it was impossible to keep this level of excitement up, and after a while, we became exhausted. It wasn't an ordinary kind of weariness, like one gets after several days of hard work, but an all-encompassing, mind-altering fatigue that pushed us past the boundaries of normal human behavior. Audie Murphy described the experience well:

> As if under the influence of some drug, I slide off the tank destroyer and, without looking back, walk down through the forest. If the Germans want to shoot me, let them. I am too weak from fear and exhaustion to care...I feel nothing: no sense of triumph;

no exhilaration at being alive. Even the
weariness seems to have passed. Existence
has taken on the quality of a dream in which
I am detached from all that is present. I
hear the shells bursting among the trees, see
the dead scattered on the ground; but I do
not connect them with anything that par-
ticularly concerns me.

This kind of numbness in combat had its bene-
fits. It protected us from fear and broke down our
resistance to the idea that we might somehow escape this world of war without a major wound or
illness or worse. The writer James Jones, who saw
some combat on Guadalcanal, called this "the evo-
lution of a soldier." The end point of this process,
says Jones, perhaps with too much drama, is "the
soldier's final full acceptance of the fact that his
name is already written down in the rolls of the
already dead." Accepting fate can be quite liberating on the battlefield.

****

Toward the end of March, Division headquarters
ordered the 2d platoon to take and hold a hilltop
that our intelligence officers named "Lovely Lady."
Lovely Lady sat on the southern tip of a horse-
shoe-shaped ridge in the Luzon interior. We
looked north across 150 yards of dense jungle valley

to the other tip of the horseshoe which was slightly higher than ours and occupied by the Japanese. To our east was the open end or top of the horseshoe. To our west was the closed end or bottom where a narrow saddle through the ridge afforded passage to the jungle valley via a switchback foot trail.

The Japanese controlled this area, and holding Lovely Lady was an important division objective. So important, we received thirty Filipino guerrillas as reinforcements. These locals were a rough and raggedy looking group that appeared to have much experience, but little training.

We arrived at the outpost after a long uphill trek, having seen Japanese on the way. Our first job was to dig foxholes on the forward and reverse slopes of the ridge. To protect us as we dug in, I temporarily positioned the guerrillas in a saddle to our north, on the opposite arm of the horseshoe. The saddle offered a clear field of fire if the Japanese should emerge from their holes and start shooting. I told our guerrilla allies to hold their spot until 1600 hours, by which time we would have finished our foxholes, and they could return and dig in under our protection.

We were still digging when we heard some fire. The Filipinos came into our perimeter ahead of schedule. They'd been ambushed while making their way back to us. No doubt they had made noise and alerted enemy soldiers crossing through the saddle west of our perimeter.

"We have two wounded and two dead," the Filipino sergeant said. "They're still there."

Harry Horne stepped forward, already buckling up his gear.

"We've got to get those wounded."

I called for volunteers, making sure to assign both our men and Filipinos to the patrol. I'd never had to carry out wounded allies.

We started out in a lousy formation. A Filipino scout and sergeant accompanied me up front with some 2d platoon men in single-file behind us. A Filipino squad began on our left but soon hooked on the tail end of the column.

The scout took us right to the wounded, and Harry quickly patched them up. They were able to walk out with us through dense jungle. We left the dead behind to retrieve later.

That night, the Japanese unleashed a torrent of machine gun fire. I was crouched down in a foxhole with our radioman, Bill Mitchell, and I called for 105mm howitzers to give us some relief. As usual, I'd previously taken care to deliver our precise coordinates, observed where various concentrations hit, and designated each location with a letter. That way, when I picked up the radio, I could request, say, concentration "G" without hav-

Radioman and saber hunter Bill Mitchell,
Somerville, MA, 1945. (*Author's Collection*)

ing to describe the position again. The shells would
then begin falling on the Japanese, and the enemy
fire would be stopped.

"Fire concentration 'G,'" I said.

A minute later, a five shell salvo exploded with

three hits inside our perimeter, 150 yards short of the Japanese. The concussion shook us some, but no one was wounded. The artillery men hadn't taken into account the variation in powder temperature that occurs when the sun goes down. What hit at a certain place at noon might not at midnight, and it didn't this time.

I jumped back on the radio.

"Stop firing! They're falling in our perimeter!"

After the shelling ceased, I talked to an artillery major I knew slightly, putting on my best mock politesse.

"I know you guys don't know where your rounds are going to hit, but next time would you please try and put some on the enemy?"

The major grew defensive, so I replied by holding down the butterfly switch on the speaking end of the phone and held it a few inches above our foxhole so he could get a big earful of really close machine gun fire. Later, in good humor, I told him how rough it was at outpost Lovely Lady, implying a comparison to the relative safety of his rear position.

"Gruenfeld, wait," asked the exasperated major, "do you hear that dripping sound?"

I bit. "No, what is it?"

"That's my ass bleeding for you."

I passed that line on to the men, and they laughed at it into the next day.

That morning it became apparent that our Filipino allies were of little help. We were eating our morning rations inside the perimeter when all of a sudden this Japanese soldier came running through the open saddle to the north with his rifle at high port, as if leading an attack. He was about 150 yards away on the other side of the deep jungle draw. My men and the guerrillas opened fire.

With the first few shots he went down briefly before scrambling up the hill toward the opposing ridge top. He was about sixty feet away from safety. Our men, about forty of them in all, kept firing and missing. Instead of shooting, I was walking up and down our line reminding them to hold their rifles steady and squeeze, not jerk the triggers. I saw a Filipino with a BAR fire a full magazine of twenty rounds at nothing. The last shot went straight up in the air. After about 200 rounds from our side, one finally hit the Japanese soldier. He dropped in knee-high grass a few feet away from the protection of the ridge top. Someone who later saw the body reported that the soldier was wearing two pairs of pants.

"If he'd worn one pair, he probably would've made it."

Later that same day, another Japanese soldier came through the saddle to our west, this one car-

rying a fifty pound tripod for an American wa-
ter-cooled machine gun. He was walking on the
foot trail through the saddle, and two or three
Filipinos manning an outpost not more than ten
yards away began firing at him. Their target disappeared, leaving behind the tripod and not so
much as a drop of blood.

At night, the guerrillas fired off and on all night
at nothing. The result was pointless noise that
kept my men awake. After the second night, I'd
had enough and radioed Colonel Barron directly
to ask him to pull the guerrillas. He agreed.

I'd been hard on them, but my heart melted a
bit at the sight of guerrillas carrying out their two
dead comrades whom we'd left near the west saddle. The corpses hung like slaughtered animals on
long poles shouldered by men on each end. As I
stood at the edge of the downhill trail, the Filipinos paraded past, each one raising a hand in
salute. It was a nice touch…as long as they weren't
trying to signal to the Japanese whom to shoot
first.

Over the next two days, we held our ground in
stifling heat and didn't have much contact with
the Japanese. We grew restless and periodically
scouted the ridge for the enemy. I headed north
to the saddle where the lone Japanese soldier had
come through. I peered over to the Japanese side

1,000 to 1,200 yards away and could barely detect one or two soldiers walking. I got into the prone position and wrapped my arm in the sling. Using my knowledge of ballistic tables, I aimed the right amount over their heads and fired several shots. I don't think I hit them, but I did make them run.

The sun bore down, and by the fourth day on Lovely Lady, we'd all but run out of water. I radioed the rear for a supply party to deliver more, along with some ammunition and food. In the meantime, to quench our thirst, we ventured out to some dead Japanese, one of them wearing the two pairs of pants, and took sips from their canteens.

The Japanese launched their biggest attack against us that day. They came down our ridge in force from the west saddle, using grenades, rifles, and at least one machine gun. We replied with much the same, and I struggled to organize our defense with low ammunition. In the middle of this firefight, a Filipino supply train arrived led by our company executive officer, Verl Shufelt. I'd traveled overseas with Shufelt when he was a twenty-five-year-old 2d lieutenant and I a nineteen-year-old buck sergeant. I ran to the carriers coming up the trail and grabbed some grenades. A fearful-looking sergeant at Verl's side was urging his boss not to go any further. Verl bravely disregarded his gutless sergeant and ordered the supplies—water, ammo, and beer, in order of priority—delivered to our perimeter. While the battle raged not 100 yards away, he calmly checked off the various items as they were dropped by the back packers. I later heard that his sergeant tried to have Shufelt court-martialed for bringing the supply train up during a firefight.

The battle grew closer, but neither side drew much blood. At one point, Ed Barker had an enemy thirty feet away. But he didn't shoot at first because he feared the soldier was a Filipino wearing Japanese gear. "You Jap? You Jap?" I heard him say before he fired into the soldier's chest. Somehow, the enemy got away but left a blood trail.

A couple days later, I figured out we'd soon be leaving Lovely Lady. I was inside the perimeter when I spotted a lone Japanese below us to the east. Without a clear field of fire, I called in some 4.2-inch chemical mortars. Forty rounds exploded in the small patch of trees he was in. I radioed confirmation.

"That should do it," I said.

"No, Gruenfeld," a mortar guy responded from a couple thousand yards away, "he's still moving."

They gave him seventy-five more rounds. That's when I knew we were being relieved. Mortar squads to the rear usually got news before we did. These mortarmen were clearly lightening their ammo load for the long trek off the line.

As we awaited relief, a forward artillery observer came up to Lovely Lady to check out the action. He had never seen live enemy before and, without alerting me, accepted the invitation of a couple of my guys to escort him to a spot along the ridge which afforded a clear view of Japanese. I saw them head toward the north saddle and decided to accompany them. One of the men had mentioned hearing some digging to the east of the north saddle, and I wanted to check it out.

I had another motive. Not long before, a fellow officer in our company who was notorious for failing to accept his fair share of danger retreated to an extra safe position when he learned his outfit would soon be relieved. Shortly after he got there, a stray artillery round landed on top of him. I saw it as poetic justice, and I wanted to demonstrate that I didn't operate that way.

As we exited the perimeter, I alerted our machine gun squad to what we were doing, just in case we needed support fire.

Coming with me was the tall lanky Ed Barker, nicknamed "Abe" by the men. Ed was a trusted partner, a deer hunter from Maine and a member of the 43d Division since its activation in 1941. While the forward observer got his view of the Japanese, Ed and I took the ridge trail and headed east.

The foot wide trail wound through a sea of eight-foot high cogan grass. Visibility was limited to five or ten yards at most. As we twisted and turned through the grass, it became still and hot. A dead calm enveloped us, and the hair on the back of my neck suddenly stood on its end. After 100 more yards, the trail gained elevation and made two switchback turns. I entered the second turn carefully in the crouched position. Rounding the corner, I stood up tall enough to see a pile of fresh dirt at the lip of a foxhole uphill about eight feet away.

I crouched back down and turned around to look at Ed. Signaling with my hands, I indicated the foxhole. I didn't know if it was occupied. I could see that the ground beyond the foxhole leveled out, but with the tall grass covering a bend in the trail I couldn't determine if there were other Japanese there too. If there were, and I raised myself high enough to look into the foxhole, I'd be a nice big target.

I weighed my options. I could turn around and slip away, and then call in mortar or artillery fire on the spot. But the foxhole might be unoccupied, and it seemed cowardly to retreat. I could try to drop a grenade into the hole, but that might alert nearby enemy to our presence. Perhaps the Japanese already knew we were there and were waiting in ambush, though Ed and I had been as silent as possible.

All these things ran through my mind in the few

seconds it took for me to settle on the aggressive course of action. Perhaps it was my need to impress the crack veteran Ed, but I decided I'd stand up, look in the hole, and be prepared to fire on any enemy further up the trail.

I plotted each move in my mind. Where I'd place my feet, how I'd hold my rifle, and how I'd pivot and even breathe as I took the three steps necessary to look into the foxhole. I pantomimed my plan to Ed. I was tight as a drum.

I breathed deep and turned uphill. I took one quick step, then another. At the third, I pivoted and pointed my rifle down into an empty foxhole. I looked up. BANG! A Japanese up the trail in another foxhole shot at me from twenty feet. He missed. I put two rounds in his upper chest, fired twice more up the trail, then turned to run.

As I headed back down the trail there was Ed, standing pat, showing heart, and providing cover with five quick shots. When I reached Ed, I turned and emptied my rifle to cover his withdrawal.

I yelled a lot in combat, most of us did, and I shouted as I ran down the trail to let our men know where we were. The machine gun squad at the perimeter came to life, laying down suppressing fire. One rifleman in our perimeter mistook us for Japanese and took a shot. He missed. Lucky again.

****

L Company, my old outfit, relieved us at Lovely Lady, and we were put into reserve in low country near a quiet village. We settled into an idyllic spot where the locals were friendly, the enemy few, and the weather mostly dry. We still slept in foxholes, but we had the luxury of time to improve them with tarps and building materials. Our scrounging also turned up some dried soup and other provisions, which our men traded to the locals for a feast of chickens, pigs, and 104 bananas.

The respite also gave me a chance to spend some time alone. After weeks of sharing a foxhole every night, I needed some solitude and so ventured out into the surrounding countryside for a solo patrol. I hiked and climbed, sneaking around as if I were back in McHenry playing cowboys and Indians. After a few hours, I ran across a beautiful spring. Looking into the crystal pool, I could see little fish swimming around and took a drink. A perfect place for a bath, I thought. It had been a long time since I was clean.

I worried about the Japanese. Surely, they'd discovered this location too and probably returned often for water. I remained vigilant and kept my rifle and grenades at the ready as I stripped down and entered the pool. The cool water enveloped me and, for a few wonderful moments, I almost forgot the war.

Turning around, I snapped out of my reverie. A young Filipina girl was just a few yards downstream collecting drinking water. Somehow she had managed to sneak up on me. If she'd been a Japanese soldier, I'd have been dead.

Not far from our reserve post were horses we had rounded up a few weeks earlier while on a nearby ridge line. They had originally belonged to an American cavalry outfit before the Japanese invaded in early 1942 and captured them. We'd seen these emaciated animals wandering around below our hilltop perch and decided to herd them our way by firing mortars to their other side. The explosions drove the horses into our lines where GI cowboys roped them in.

Now they were tied up in a bombed-out building that served as a stable. I'd been on horses before a few times and thought it would be fun to take one for a gallop. I picked out the best-looking beast and hoisted myself up.

We thundered through a coconut grove toward a rice paddy I wanted to cross. The horse hit its stride as we approached the edge of the paddy and then, without warning, made a sharp ninety degree turn to the left, nearly throwing me clean off his back.

I hung upside down on the horse with my hands around its neck. The horse kept running until my feet finally left the stirrups. Then, it stopped abruptly. I dropped to the ground, and carefully remounted him.

I learned later that cavalry horses are so smart and well-trained, they know better than to enter a rice paddy where the footing is bad. Now chastened, I trotted, rather than galloped, back to the ersatz stable. As we drew toward the building, the horse headed straight toward a low-hanging joist and ducked his head. The joist hit me square in the chest, knocking the wind out of me and allowing the horse to continue on solo. I was left hanging doubled-over the joist, while my men roared with laughter.

The rest gave several of us a chance to spend a couple days in Manila. Barker and Daley accompanied me in a jeep, along with a couple other noncoms.

Once the Pearl of the Orient, Manila was now a city of rubble. The Japanese had leveled as many buildings and killed as many civilians as they could before evacuating. GIs swarmed all over, fighting, stealing, and drinking. We weren't permitted to bring our rifles into the city, and that made us nervous. So we carried big knives and some grenades. It was like the Wild West. A GI we met in a bar warned us to keep an eye on our jeep.

"They'll steal it right from under your nose," he

said. One driver pulled from his pocket a distributor cap. Displaying it proudly, he explained that he always removed the engine part when he left his jeep so that no one could drive it away.

GI lore had it that "Gen. Alabama Swing and his Ten Thousand Thieves" were to blame for the stolen jeep epidemic. We knew paratroopers had a lot to do with it.

After a couple of hours at the bar, we looked outside and saw a gang of Filipinos pushing a jeep down the street even though it lacked a distributor cap. Our friend in the bar chased after them.

We stepped outside into the bright sun and walked to the banks of the Pasig River, which ran through the middle of the city. We stripped down and jumped in. It felt good to swim again, and I tested myself against the current. I swam toward a bridge a good distance away. As I swam above the bridge, I saw a distinct shape in a backwater: the bloated corpse of a Japanese soldier, one arm jutting grotesquely out of the water. I quickly swam back to our starting point and climbed out.

The next day, we boarded our jeep and returned to our reserve area.

"You know," said one of the noncoms, "this rest is nice, but it's not shortening the war any. I'll be glad to get back up on the line." His buddy agreed.

I was happy to hear them say it.

****

We returned to combat on April 3 as one of the lead elements of a rare night attack. It was a bold and complicated maneuver that involved getting tanks, medium artillery, antiaircraft guns, demolition crews, and the entire 103d Regiment into position on the jungle slopes of Mount Sembrano without being detected by the Japanese. The objective was Mabitac in the Santa Maria Valley on the eastern side of Laguna de Bay. After the collapse of the southern Shimbu Line, the Japanese had withdrawn to the hillsides and valley villages connected by a trail network and north-south highway.

Trekking into enemy terrain at night put us on edge. For the first time, we had a Nisei interpreter with us. In addition to interrogating prisoners, this Japanese American soldier helped to scout the area.

We paused at our assembly point and awaited the signal to attack at 0300. Peering into the early morning light, I saw something crawling—it looked like the head of an enemy soldier--and fired. The movement stopped. I'd killed a pig.

We swept down the hills and across rice paddies into Mabitac. A surprised Japanese sentry ran up the town's main street yelling to alert his comrades. The enemy scattered into the countryside.

As the morning light spread, the Nisei inter-preter and I scouted a trail that ran through a nearby coconut grove. Moving quietly between the trees, I spotted a man about 200 yards away leaving a little cluster of shacks. He had some women with him. I got into the prone position behind a log and peered through my sight. He was definitely Japanese.

Though in a steady position, I was worried about shooting a woman, so I carefully chose my target. The Nisei crouched beside me as I squeezed the trigger. The enemy soldier disappeared, along with the women. I returned to our post not knowing if I'd gotten him.

We moved our lines to the east that afternoon, while the Nisei interpreter joined a unit that shifted north, past the uphill trail where I'd taken the shot. That evening, we sat in our newly dug foxholes eating our dinner rations. The Nisei came into our perimeter. He'd gone back to the coconut grove where I'd shot at the enemy soldier.

"That was a great shot, Lieutenant," he said. "You got that guy."

The men clapped my back and congratulated me with the usual litany of obscenities.

"Way to go, Jay. You got another one of those yellow cocksuckers!"

"File another notch!"

"Yeah," the Nisei chimed in, "You shot him through the lungs. He died reading his Bible."

A deathly quiet descended on the group. No more

than one percent of the Japanese Army was Christian, and I'd found one on a mountain trail. For the first time, the enemy seemed really human.

We didn't talk about it afterward, but the platoon wasn't the same. We moved on to other ridges in other foxholes, but for a while we were no longer "The Fighting Deuce." We were just a bunch of Americans kids camping out in a jungle. It took about a week for our shells to harden again and for us to regain the tough veteran countenance that betrays no regret at death dealing.

Our platoon had just returned to normal when, all of a sudden, a lone Japanese soldier appeared in plain view on a trail about 150 yards away from our ridgeline foxholes.

"Nobody shoot," I ordered in a hushed voice. "We'll get all set, and when I count four, we'll fire all together."

At four, twenty rifles opened up, and the lone walker fell away from the trail.

No one cheered. The silence bespoke our discomfort with the execution.

"That wasn't very sporting," Briones finally said. "That poor little guy didn't know what hit him."

The body lay untouched by our platoon. We noticed the wild horses avoiding the spot, as if spooked by the executed enemy.

****

One night we were being moved from one part of the line to another. We'd been promised three days rest but only got one-and-a-half, so the men were owly. They'd seen, once again, how well the rear echelon troops had it: clean clothes, plenty of beer, women, and zero danger. Now we had to head right back into combat, while they got to play. I was riding in the cab of a deuce-and-a-half truck. My platoon was assembled in the back.

We passed slowly through the middle of a small town whose streets were crammed with rear echelon soldiers and their Filipina girls. They were all dressed up laughing and grabbing under street corner lights. I heard my guys trading barbs with the partying GIs. The back-and-forth grew more heated as we made our way through town. By the time we neared the town limits, the two sides were shouting at each other.

At the last lighted intersection, one of my men— I never found out who—stood up, pulled the pin on a hand grenade, yelled "Grenade!" and tossed it into the crowd. The partiers panicked, diving for drainage ditches and climbing over each other to escape. The grenade popped innocuously (the TNT had been removed) as my men howled with laughter. On hearing the story, I couldn't help but laugh with them. God knows they deserved a good laugh. But I also worried that someone might report the truck number and that I'd get chewed out, but good.

We arrived at our new outpost, near Mabitac in a brushy part of the Santa Maria Valley. I was surly. We had no clear orders except to protect a hardtop road and, to make matters worse, we once again had a Filipino guerrilla unit attached to us. I told the guerrillas that if they kept us awake by firing at night, they'd be sorry.

We did little except run routine security patrols. The men relaxed a little too much. I caught two guys playing cards on guard duty, one of them the jerk whose bullets had hit behind our men working on the nine suicide cave. I chewed them out royally. Soon after, Lieutenant Colonel Barron came into our perimeter to find out what we were doing.

"Have you patrolled up around these hills?" he asked, waving his hand.

"No, sir," I responded. "We haven't had any orders."

The colonel told me to expect a major patrol soon.

Perhaps because of this unusual lull in combat activity, Headquarters Company sent a *Time* magazine reporter to meet with us. I suppose someone decided we made good copy.

"What's he going to write about?" we asked each other. "We're not doing anything."

Harry Horne suggested we simulate a night attack complete with grenades and automatic fire. I vetoed the idea.

The correspondent was Gilbert Cant, a senior editor of *Time*. His visit turned out to be a pleasure and not just for the hot meals that accompanied his arrival. He seemed genuinely to enjoy our company and appreciate our efforts in the field. He entertained us with stories from his journeys through the Pacific and especially with covering Douglas MacArthur at his headquarters in Hollandia, New Guinea. On the morning of Cant's departure, I asked him if the General was as much a showboat as everyone said.

"Jay," Cant replied with his hand on my shoulder, "the stage's greatest loss was when MacArthur decided to go to West Point."

The men enjoyed that comment.

Soon after Cant's visit, we got orders for an all-day patrol. The southward route took us from the valley floor up a steep mountain trail into large old-growth timber. The terrain was unlike anything I'd seen on Luzon. These weren't the usual coconuts and palms but big 100 foot deciduous hardwoods—lauan or "Philippine mahogany"—with fluted buttress bases rising out of a carpet of moss. I hadn't realized how much I missed big trees.

We reached the mountain's peak, and fog rolled

in. It was so thick we wandered through a saddle, and, when the fog receded, found ourselves on the wrong side of the mountain. After we'd gotten our bearings, we took a break. I looked over at the lauan and turned to Daley.

"I'm going to take a solo hike over there," I said, pointing at a faint trail that led off to the east. "I'll be about fifteen or twenty minutes. I just want to see if I can find enemy signs."

The Japanese were in the area, I knew, and I walked as quietly as I could, but my focus was as much on the trees as the enemy. This was "high forest" timber with few branches down low and crowns that interlaced far above filtering the light and giving a cathedral effect. It was quiet and peaceful. I was in heaven.

I heard a faint sound up the trail, a quiet rustling. I quickly stepped behind the closest tree, which was on my right. That meant I had to look to the left of the tree to see the trail. This was a problem for I shot right-handed. I released the safety on my rifle and brought it to the ready, peaking up the trail.

The noise came into view. A large blue and gray bird with a bright white chest waddled with dignity down the trail. In the center of the white was a brilliant scarlet patch that looked exactly like a bloody wound. I stood mesmerized at this magnificent creature until it strutted off the trail into the timber. It was only after the war when, looking through the University of Illinois library, I discovered what it was: a Bleeding Heart Pigeon.

****

The left or southern flank of the Shimbu Line was now completely demolished. Many enemy soldiers not killed or captured over the previous six weeks had removed north to the towering hills surrounding the Ipo Dam on the Angat River.

The Ipo Dam stronghold proved more formidable than expected. The 112th Cavalry Regiment tried and failed to take it, reporting heavy and accurate use of artillery against their slightest movements. Japanese antiaircraft guns prevented good aerial reconnaissance, and enemy night patrols harassed our outposts. Throughout April, we pounded the position with artillery and air bombardments to no effect. With the dam's gates closed and Manila's water supply in peril, General Krueger decided that the Ipo Dam would have to be taken the hard way and chose the 43d Division to do it.

What made the Ipo Dam offensive especially difficult was the terrain. The Japanese heavily defended the one mountain road leading to the site, so our battle plan had us attacking from the south where there were no roads, nor hardly even trails, only a bare range of rocky hills guarded over by artillery, mortars, and machine guns. With rainy season coming on, bulldozers would have to work doubletime to get our artillery into position. Even if the attack succeeded, we'd lose a lot of men.

We enjoyed a short rest at Antipolo. Harry Horne came down with hepatitis and was sent back to Manila for treatment. It nearly broke his heart to leave us, though he knew he was going back to safety and a warm dry bunk. I'd miss Harry quite a bit and composed some doggerel in his honor:

> If ever you were wounded and needed expert care,
> Our crazy Johnstown medic would reach you anywhere.
> Many had the Silver Star for doing less than he,
> And if the wounded gave 'em,
> He'd sure have more than three.

Harry's understudy was Bert Johnson, a twenty-one-year-old single guy from Richmond, California. Bert would serve as our medic for the upcoming offensive.

We also got a new company commander, Captain Taylor. Taylor was a staff officer with no combat experience. His predecessor had been wounded, and the division was now scouring the rear for frontline officers. Such men often made good combat leaders, but Taylor seemed unwilling or unable to seek counsel from his subordinates. He never asked me anything.

Taylor started us out under cover of darkness on May 3. This was to be a surprise attack, and we were not to alert the enemy to our movements. When our bulldozers worked making roads, we fired artillery to cover the sound. We were assigned to the extreme right flank of a massive operation that required the precise coordination of each battalion.

We hadn't gotten far when suddenly two machine guns opened up on the lead platoon. We hit the ground and sought cover. I looked up to find the source of the fire and recognized immediately the tracer bullets. They were dark in color and therefore most likely ours. Japanese tracers were almost always lighter.

"I think those are our guys shooting at us," I thought, assuming that Taylor would soon straighten things out.

Instead, we passed the first night of our long hike to the Ipo Dam assembly point pinned down by our own men. We were all tired and, to my surprise, everyone fell asleep. Everyone but me, that is. I couldn't understand how we could be so close to the enemy and not have guards out. I woke up a sergeant, and he shook awake some men for guard duty.

The next morning the Fighting Deuce took the lead, and I sent our scouts up the trail. No sooner had we started than our battalion commander, Colonel Barron, stormed up behind me, not saying a word, brushing past me, then the scouts. In full fury and disregarding the danger that lay ahead, the colonel effectively led our company on a fast march.

I could tell right away what had happened. Learning we had been stopped by our own machine guns, our regimental commander Colonel Cleland had no doubt chewed out Barron, who then chewed out Taylor for stalling the operation needlessly. Chastised and woefully behind schedule, Barron was now determined to make up for lost time. We hiked at top speed just to keep up, hoofing it through rugged country to get to where we should have been all along.

We finally made it before dark. That night, I dug in with Captain Taylor.

We didn't talk of the machine gun snafu, but mainly of sports and his native Pacific Northwest, land of large trees. Taylor owned a sporting goods store back home. Our foxhole was spacious and comfortable, as foxholes go, with a poncho overhead to keep the rain out and a flask of brandy to warm him. He offered me a swig, my first and only drink of hard liquor in combat, and it burned going down.

The next day we set out to our final position on the extreme right. We received fire as we moved, long distance at first, but late in the day a machine gun narrowly missed our scouts, and we sought cover. There we were, pinned down again.

Both our radio men, Chuck Wakeley and Bill Mitchell, were at Taylor's side. My platoon was about 100 yards to the right.

"Go up there and see what's going on," Taylor said, pointing to a knob where the scouts had received the fire.

"I don't want to do that, Captain," Wakeley responded. "It's exposed to where the machine gun is."

Taylor looked annoyed, and, as if to say, "I'll do it myself," got up and climbed to the knob.

He was feeling the pressure. He'd screwed up once and got chewed out for it. He was determined not to get bogged down again. He acted as though he didn't know the situation was different this time. This fire was coming from a Nambu machine gun, not one of ours.

Taylor stood up on the knob and looked around. Within seconds a machine gun burst stitched him from torso to head. Taylor became our company's first killed in the Ipo Dam offensive.

The main attack began at 2200 that night. A feinting maneuver by our 169th Regiment to the north made the enemy at first think the attack was coming on the mountain highway, the only easy approach to the dam. Our objective was to take possession of the critical ridgeline to the south of the dam before the Japanese could figure out what was happening and reinforce it. So, over several days, we hiked, then hiked some more. We picked our way through the hills sometimes in the moonlight, advancing 5,000 yards. Artillery began landing, but still we trekked 8,000 more yards. The regiment seized Hill 1400, then quickly moved north to Hill 1410, then Hill 1000. We needed to capture these positions so that the 118th Engineer Battalion could build roads and bridges, and allow our artillery to be brought to bear on the enemy.

As we moved, we got word that Lieutenant Colonel Barron had been relieved of command of our battalion. Barron, it was rumored, had refused an order from Colonel Cleland, his superior. Cleland wanted Barron to move a unit of his 100 yards forward. The regimental commander was seeking the appearance of progress, a pin move on map at division headquarters. But shifting a perimeter 100 yards meant that tired men had to give up their foxholes and dig news ones, robbing them of precious rest. Rumor had it that Barron wouldn't make his men do it and so was sacked. I took Barron's side, of course, and regretted losing a fine leader.

The division's firepower was in evidence in those early days of the offensive as artillery units pummeled enemy positions ahead of our advance. Dive bombers periodically swept down to destroy anti-aircraft guns, causing loud explosions. The Japanese, we later learned, were mostly ensconced in caves and thus safe from the bombardments, but the show of force built our confidence.

The enemy had now caught on to the direction of our attack and unleashed their big guns, ranging from 75mm to 150mm. Hundreds of rounds fell especially on elements of our 172d Regiment, which moved in to reinforce Hill 815, which our battalion had captured on May 12. We kept pushing north to seize one final piece of terrain, Hill 860, before we closed in on the dam. We knew if the Japanese could hold Hill 860 before us, the entire Ipo Dam operation might fail.

Rain started falling in sheets on May 13. We were now but a mile from the Ipo Dam. The closer we got, the less our own artillery was there to support us. Our guns simply grew quiet. Through my binocular, I spotted some Japanese artillerymen move a 75mm field piece into position and camouflage it. I had the exact coordinates and radioed back to have it destroyed. Nothing. Pretty soon, we'd lose our mortars too.

The Fighting Deuce began hiking toward Hill 860 in the pre-dawn hours of May 14. We'd been on the move for about ten days, grabbing sleep for a couple hours at a time when we could. Our fatigues were now caked in mud. There were no towns, no villages, and hardly any trees. Nothing marked the land except strange rock formations. These outcroppings, writes Army historian Robert Ross Smith, lent the area "an oppressive, weird aspect" and "wild, desolate beauty." "Some stretching horizontally across the land, some pyramiding dizzily to sudden, jumbled heights," Smith continues, "these dark grayish outcroppings and sharp pinnacles looked like the product of a fantastic nightmare induced by studying a Dali portraiture of the moon's surface."

Our route to Hill 860 took the platoon between two towering verticals of rock spaced about fifteen yards apart. When I saw them, I slowed down. The hair on my neck stood on end. This is the perfect place for an ambush, I thought. My scouts, just ahead of me, approached the rocks. I warned them to be extra careful, and if it appeared too risky to avoid the pass. But they showed no fear and kept walking straight through. Being the fearless leader, I said nothing of my ominous feeling and followed them. We made it through without incident. Perhaps my instincts were starting to fail me. Perhaps, after over four months of combat, I was getting spooked.

Another company had gotten to Hill 860 before us and had dug in on the reverse side of the peak. We relieved them. As they were heading out, the guys warned us that the enemy kept our position under constant surveillance and fired at anyone showing above the crest. That didn't keep my men from almost immediately crawling to the ridge top and begin taking shots at visible Japanese. I didn't urge them to do this. They were just living up to the reputation of the Fighting Deuce.

I hung back for a while and then decided to join the crew on the ridge top. I took up a position just to the left of a rock ledge that gave good protection. I used my binocular to observe the enemy positions. Clearly visible on the crest of an opposing ridge about 600 yards away was a large caliber Japanese machine gun called a Type 98. It was classed as an antiaircraft-antitank gun, though it was being used against our infantry. The gun crew was loading 20mm shells into the top of a curved eighteen-inch magazine and then firing about ninety degrees from my position. I took two shots at the crew, and they turned the gun on me.

I ducked my head behind the rock ledge. The velocity of their bullets was relatively slow, and there was a definite lag between the time I saw the smoke at the muzzle and when the bullets cracked by. This lag time was my ally. If the gun's bullets traveled at 2,200 feet per second, it would take them approximately eight-tenths of a second to reach me. A fast runner could go eight yards in that time, and all I had to do was duck my head.

I was about to lock into this duel with the machine gun when one of the men called out to me.

"There's a Nip down to your left!"

I looked downhill to the left. A lone Japanese soldier was sitting contentedly outside his cave eating his rations. He was only about 125 yards away.

"Get him," I told the man who had spotted him.

"I can't," he responded. "I can't shoot at him without exposing myself to that machine gun. But I can see him with my telescope and still be under cover. I'll spot for you."

Things were now complicated.

In order to shoot at the Japanese eating outside the cave, I had to rise up to a kneeling position with my weight on both knees. When I did that, I'd be silhouetted against the skyline. The Type 98

I first returned to the Philippines in 1964 and hiked to the spot where I spent my last day and took this photograph. Note the bare hillside. The grass was even shorter in 1945. (*Author's collection*)

gunner would have a perfect shot at me. Firing from the kneeling position was also awkward. It would be tough to get off a good shot. Nevertheless, as fearless leader, I felt required to try it. So, I did.

I could see the big magazine on the top of the machine gun and tell which direction it was firing. When the magazine was pointing away from me, I rose to my knees and fired at the ration eater. Didn't get him. So, I tried again, and then again. I expected him to slump over from a hit or at least take cover. But this hungry Japanese just kept eating, blithely ignoring my attempts to take him out.

Could I be that far off? I wondered. Sure, I was

a little wobbly, but I was hitting close. Finally, I grew desperate. With the machine gun turned toward me, I saw the muzzle smoke. I rose to my knees, took a shot, and ducked behind the ledge. Bullets whizzed by.

I'd fired eight shots, and my rifle was now empty. My spotter issued his report.

"Eight rounds and the son-of-a-bitch is still eating his lunch. And you were supposed to be such a great shot," he said in disgust.

It was May 14, my eighty-ninth day with the Fighting Deuce and the day I lost my shooting rep. I didn't know it, but I had only one more day to endure the ribbing.

I continued firing, finally hitting the magazine of the machine gun and perhaps killing the gunner. I fired about seventy rounds on that ridge top and, for the first time during my war, fell asleep in my foxhole that night without cleaning my rifle after having used it.

Looking back, I'm almost glad I didn't kill that hungry Japanese soldier. Not because of compassion, but because I've enjoyed telling that story so much over the years.

CHAPTER SEVEN

The Journey Home

By the following evening, I had finally earned my Purple Hearts and had spent my last day as an active warrior, my ninetieth as leader of the Fighting Deuce. Midnight found me in a tent camp that served as our battalion aid station. I lay on my cot and watched the tent fill up with wounded. The Fighting Deuce was virtually wiped out. Only eight were left.

A company's worth of Filipino litter bearers arrived to deliver us to the nearest road, a journey of eight hours by foot. We proceeded in total darkness, one man at each corner of each litter, trudging silently in single file. Our grand parade of wounded and their guards wound its way through a maze of hills. We were nervous and perfectly aware that one Japanese machine gun hidden in a cave could dispatch the lot of us in a few minutes.

Every hour or so, we stopped to rest. At one stop, my litter bearers lowered me hard on a tree stump, gouging my hip wound. I moaned in agony.

The sky began to brighten. A couple hours later, we approached the road, which was nothing but a narrow strip of knee-deep mud. The first GI I saw was our battalion chaplain, Webster, who went through the ranks of litters greeting each man. Webster was the type of chaplain who exposed himself to combat and saw to it the living and the dead were properly tended to, no matter the conditions. He reached me.

"Gruenfeld, I didn't think they could get you!" he exclaimed with characteristic cheer.

Sometime that afternoon, our regimental commander, Colonel Joseph Cleland, arrived at the aid station for a meeting. I watched him for hours. He never once came by to talk with any of the wounded. That bothered me. It bothered me a lot. I thought of Lieutenant Colonel Barron, the brave leader he relieved of duty.

The litter bearers loaded me onto a jeep next to Brumfield. The road was so impassable that a bulldozer towed the jeep to a drier section where ambulances waited to take us to a field hospital. Brumfield and I shared an ambulance. There, a medic prepared a blood transfusion. "Poor Brum," I said to myself, "he's worse off than I thought."

Then, the medic stuck me with the needle. I was the one in worse shape, it turned out.

Tractors had dragged a portable surgical hospital through the mud until they got stuck, still far from the front. This is where we took turns undergoing surgery. There was no separate operating room or partition. We simply lay on our cots or on the ground watching doctors hack away at the men who came before us until it was our turn. A surgeon gave me sodium pentothal and told me to count to ten. I took it as a personal challenge and tried counting to twenty. I didn't make it to two.

I awoke to Brum describing how they "chopped away at my hip." My wound received the designation "FCC"—"fractured compound comminuted." Part of my ilium, or hip, was broken into several fragments. The gunshot wound to my arm now had a bandage sticking clear through it to facilitate an even healing.

After a day or two in the field hospital, we were sent to a church in Manila. Cots filled the sanctuary. We were still largely caked with mud, even after having been operated on, and Filipina girls came around to bathe us. They were young and beautiful, and I hardly complained about the poor job they did. Much mud was more or less spread around, rather than wiped off.

I now finally had the opportunity to reflect on

my last day and decided to put Bert Johnson in for a decoration. I had in mind the Distinguished Service Cross or Silver Star, the second and third highest awards in the United States Army. I composed a letter to Captain Galyea on Bert's behalf:

May 20, 1945
Manila Hospital
Subject: Recommendation for the Award of Silver Star or DSC to Pfc. Bert Johnson (Medic)
In the Ipo Dam area of Luzon, 15 May, time 1700, the 2d and 3d platoons of Company C 103d Infantry, were in the attack. Casualties were heavy. Pfc. Johnson, 2d platoon medic, while exposed to heavy small arms fire risked his life time after time giving first aid to seven wounded men. Johnson also supervised and took part in the evacuation of the severely wounded men. Although wounded in the shoulder early in the fight, Johnson stayed in the fight and continued to give aid to the wounded.

Johnson's daring actions doubtless saved the lives of some of his fellow soldiers and he was a magnificent example for the men around him. His heroic behavior was far above and beyond the call of duty.

Being one of the severely wounded men I was an eye witness to Pfc. Johnson's actions and certify to the truth of the above statements.

J. Jay Gruenfeld, 2d Lt.
Platoon Leader, 2d Plt.

Later I learned that my letter got lost. Captain Galyea ended up with the Silver Star. Bert got nothing, not even a promotion. This type of injustice, inexcusable though it was, wasn't uncommon. Too often what hardly gets noticed when done by a private received commendation when done by an officer.

I was put on a Dutch liner converted into a hospital ship, the S.S. *Maetsuycker*, for a 1,500 mile journey to Biak Island north of New Guinea. Just prior to boarding, a medic gave me a final once over, along with Virgil Brumfield, Bill Mitchell, and a few others. "What is this some kind of an elite unit?" he asked. "These guys only want to know how soon they can get back into combat." I felt proud.

I was surprised to see the *Maetsuycker* festooned with flags, a big red cross, and lights even at night. By this stage of the war, the Japanese respected hospital ships.

More surgery awaited me at the Army hospital on Biak. They cleaned the wound and removed some bone fragments. I was finally healed enough to sit in a wheelchair.

Bill Mitchell and Virgil Brumfield were in the same hospital, and they often visited me in the officers ward. The first time they came in I noticed that while Mitch was walking well, he looked gray and had a cough. I turned him so that the bullet exit and entry holes were lined up and using my limited knowledge of anatomy said, "Are they sure that bullet didn't get your lung?" Mitch replied that the x-ray didn't indicate that. It was only later, back in the States, when he learned that he'd been walking around with a bullet-collapsed lung and pneumonia.

Brum was on crutches and said his knee "hurt like hell." The bullet had broken a bone, and eventually, in the States, he'd get a big cast. Another one of my men, Don Brookhart, was also there on crutches with a bullet wound to the foot just below the ankle. Don was a replacement soldier I hadn't known well, and I enjoyed talking with him about his days as a rodeo cowboy before the war. He was a fine soldier and nice guy.

Mitch, Brum, Brookhart, and I shared a new kind of camaraderie on Biak. We all enjoyed the good fortune of having survived combat and the satisfaction of knowing we'd done a good job. My days in that hospital were some of the best of my life. When the doctor told me I was going to be "evacuated" back home, my combat maturity left me for a few seconds, and I must have sounded like a kid as I laughed and shouted for joy.

From Biak, I began a six-day 10,000 mile journey aboard a four-engine Douglas airplane, a C-54, that took me to Manila, Kwajalein, Guam,

Johnson Island, Hawaii, and finally California. On one of those flights, I took my first steps since being wounded. I needed to use the head and, not wanting a bedpan and not asking the nurse for help, I simply stood up and limped back. I guess it was the beginning of my rehabilitation.

We landed at Fairfield-Suisun Army Air Base (now Travis Air Force Base) in between Fairfield and Sacramento. I'd never seen California and won't ever forget catching sight of those golden hills when we landed. While being processed for shipment to Nichols General Hospital in Louisville, Kentucky, I was told I was put in for a Silver Star. Also, I had no officer serial number. The only things I brought back with me were a shirt and pair of pants. I'd nothing else, no gear, no dog tags, not even underwear. It took a while, but by the time I boarded an eastbound train in late June, I had a serial number. Nothing came of the Silver Star.

In Ward 35 of Nichols Hospital, I had the good fortune of being assigned a bed next to that of Evart "Hank" Henry, a fellow battlefield commissioned 2d lieutenant who'd been wounded on Luzon within a week of me. Hank was a relatively ancient thirty-two years old, a kind of big brother with whom I shared an instant connection. Besides being a rifle platoon leader, Hank was an avid hunter, fisherman, and athlete, so we had much to talk about over the next several months. He told me that his eagerness to get overseas and into combat was so great that he endured the pain of a slipped disc, rather than reporting on sick-call, so that he could join the 37th Division on Bougainville.

He told me another story that encapsulates the bonding of combat infantry. One of Hank's scouts was a tough little guy named Nicky Ermon. Nicky, though a good soldier, was a constant and articulate griper about the unfairness of the infantry's lot: the lousy food, the exhaustion, and the constant danger. Nicky prayed openly for a golden wound that would send him to the safety of the rear but not maim him for life. One day he got his wish, suffering a through-and-through bullet wound in his arm. As he left for the rear, he waved the wounded arm saying, "Goodbye you poor bastards! You'll never see me again! USA, here I come!"

Two weeks later, Nicky returned to his unit, his arm still full of puss and far from healed.

"Nicky, how come you came back?" asked the wide-eyed Hank.

"Hank, you guys are the only real family I've ever had. I missed the platoon and went AWOL from the hospital to get back here."

Hank and I talked much of our love for combat infantry, and both of us were delighted when my dad sent me a copy of *Up Front*, the best-selling book by Army sergeant and cartoonist Bill Mauldin. I'd seen some of Mauldin's terrific combat cartoons, but not nearly as much as the guys in Europe did. Mauldin was rifleman in the 45th Division who'd worked his way on to the Army newspaper *Stars & Stripes* during the Italian campaign and won a Pulitzer Prize in May 1945. He'd joined the prewar Army and understood infantry life from the ground up. His cartoons did in pictures what Ernie Pyle's columns did in words: they gave the folks back home a glimpse of the world of combat while boosting the morale of those in the foxholes. He was our champion.

Hank and I laughed at the cartoons, but the prose of *Up Front* was an unexpected surprise. Mauldin was lyrical especially about the fatigue that infantry combat entailed and challenged readers to simulate the experience:

> Dig a hole in your back yard while it's raining. Sit in the hole until the water climbs up around your ankles. Pour cold mud down your shirt collar. Sit there for forty-eight hours, and, so there is no danger of your dozing off, imagine that a guy is sneaking

"I'm beginnin' to feel like a fugitve from th' law of averages."

Audie Murphy described himself "as a fugitive from the law of averages," a feeling shared by all combat soldiers. This caption is the only quotation by Mauldin to appear in *The Oxford Dictionary of Quotations*. (*Courtesy Bill Mauldin Estate, LLC*) around waiting for a chance to club you on the head or set your house on fire.

Get out of the hole, fill a suitcase full of rocks, pick it up, put a shotgun in your other hand and walk on the muddiest road you can find. Fall flat on your face every few minutes as you imagine big meteors streaking down to sock you.

After ten or twelve miles (remember, you are still carrying the shotgun and the suitcase) start sneaking through the wet brush. Imagine the somebody has booby-trapped your route with rattlesnakes which will bite you if you step on them. Give some friend a shotgun and have him blast in your direction once in a while.

Snoop around until you find a bull. Try to figure out a way to sneak around him without letting him see you. When he does see you, run like hell all the way back to your hole in the back yard, drop the suitcase and shotgun, and get in.

If you repeat this performance every three days for several months you may begin to understand why an infantryman sometimes gets out of breath. But you still won't understand how he feels when things get tough.

Many years later, in 2002, I tried to contact him and discovered through his son that the great cartoonist was ailing in a nursing home with some form of dementia. He didn't speak and didn't seem to recognize friends or family. He wasn't getting any visitors. It seemed a shame that a man who was a hero to combat infantrymen in World War II should be alone. So, one afternoon, I drove 200 miles to Park Superior Nursing Home in Newport Beach to sit with Bill.

I talked with him, told him how much he meant to me, and then, at the end of the visit, pinned a replica of a Combat Infantry Badge on his pajamas. Bill looked down at the pin, looked up at me, and beamed a big beautiful smile. I said, "Bill, do you want me to come back?" And Bill responded with the first word he'd spoken in weeks: "Yes."

I contacted Bill's son and told him that if we could get a little publicity, infantry veterans would clamor for a chance to visit Mauldin. The family agreed. I got hold of Gordon Dillow at the *Orange County Register*, spread the word through VFWs and American Legions, and, sure enough, old warriors with their caps and memorabilia began lining the halls of the nursing home to sit with Mauldin. Bob Greene of the *Chicago Tribune* wrote a syndicated column about the phenomenon, and soon hundreds of cards and letters began pouring in to Bill. So many came that the family couldn't even open them all. By the time Bill died in January 2003, over 10,000 pieces of mail had arrived at Park Superior. A well-deserved send-off for a great man.

****

I stayed at Nichols General Hospital from late June to December and underwent a few more operations. A cute little nurse took care of me, and we enjoyed a brief innocent affair. She had a boyfriend who'd lost an eye in Europe, and I felt guilty about that.

The nurse helped me to go AWOL so I could catch a train and see my parents. I'd talked with them over the phone and had heard my mom cry, but it was a joy to see them in person again. I told them few details and none of the grim realities of my combat experiences, but I have a feeling my dad understood. After a couple days in Chicago, the nurse telegraphed me to get back as soon as possible. I had surgery scheduled and needed to be there. I arrived in Louisville dead tired and went immediately to the operating room for my final procedure on my hip. I rehabilitated myself with vigorous exercise and basketball games.

My primary infirmity was malaria, which I came down with soon after arriving at Nichols General Hospital. Hank had the same problem. After being wounded, we had stopped taking atabrine, and the malaria parasite eventually caused symptoms. The malaria attacks re-occurred for a few years. The last came in 1948 while I was a forestry student at Colorado A&M. I had a 105 degree fever and the shakes but took a Geology test before rushing off to catch a train home for Christmas break. Most of the students knew what was going on with me as I trembled in the classroom. I turned in my paper early and as I left the room I called out in a loud quivering voice, "Meeer-rry Chris-ss-mas!" It got a good laugh.

In December, the Army released me from Nichols Hospital and sent me to Camp Carson, Colorado, for convalescence. I accepted a third Purple Heart for my three minor wounds. I got to see my old girlfriend, Carol Kling, and swim four or five days a week at a fancy hotel for therapy. After a couple months, I was finally given terminal leave and then discharged from the Army at Fort Sheridan in March 1946, three years after my induction.

Later that year, our old medic Harry Horne wrote a letter from his home in Johnstown, Pennsylvania, where he was managing a B.F. Goodrich distributorship. He explained how he'd been evacuated to Manila with hepatitis when he heard about C Company being hit hard at the Ipo Dam. He couldn't sleep that night in his warm dry bunk

A happy survivor of war, I posed for this photograph while convalescing at Camp Carson, Colorado. I'd be discharged a short time later. (*Author's collection*)

while his comrades were wet and dying up in the hills. He wandered the city all the next day looking for survivors. He found Chuck Wakeley on a casualty list in a hospital, and the radioman told Harry the whole story of the Ipo Dam offensive, who made it and who didn't.

"Well the war ended when I was here in Johnstown on leave," Harry explained, "and I knew then that I would never return to the outfit. I knew that it was all over and that started me thinking, the war ended too soon for me and it was quite a blow. I knew then that I would never hear the thunder of artillery again, knew that never would I get a chance to see all the gang together. So it was over and a good thing at that."

Harry continued, "When I got home I never got accustomed to people again, especially the family, people bore me to death. For instance, my aunt just called and invited me to a D.A.R. tea tomorrow afternoon, but I will not attend. The only relaxation I find is in conversation with an old infantry man, usually in some quiet cocktail lounge pondering over a drink. These are the only people that I understand."

I imagine a lot of infantry veterans felt the same way.

****

Every combat veteran has at least one story he keeps to himself until something compels him to tell it. Chalmus Brammer, my L Company comrade who was with me on my rice paddy battle outside of Pozorrubio, told me the complete story of his second wounding fifty-six years after it occurred. All prior versions had no religious aspect.

Bram and another sergeant had made a night attack on a hut that held several enemy and a couple of women. Bram and his partner operated at night in order to get closer to the hut and not hurt the women. About twenty support troops were seventy-five yards away. A firefight broke out at close range. Bram and the sergeant had made a couple of kills when a bullet severed the big artery in Bram's thigh.

As he lay bleeding badly in the dark and rain within twenty-five feet of the remaining Japanese, Bram prayed that he would have one more chance to see his sweetheart, Peggy. Then, he says, he saw Jesus. It was just Jesus' head, silent and unmoving. Bram was comforted by the vision and knew he'd survive. His leg swelled and caused a natural tourniquet. The bleeding stopped. His squad put down heavy fire and dragged him to safety. He recovered fully except for a bad limp. (Bram and his wife of sixty-four years passed recently, within a few months of each other. Chris, his son, said they had a sixty-four-year love affair.)

****

Rex Allison, a forester and my best non-family friend when he passed in 1984, was a WWII forward observer in the 104th Infantry Division. He was captured three times and escaped twice. His normal weight was about 170 pounds, but he weighed 87 pounds when liberated.

Late in the war he was in a group of 125 officers being marched across Poland by their German captors. One of the prisoners was the senior colonel in the U.S. Army. The prisoners were near starvation on one meager meal per day that was fed before the all-day march. One morning the Germans were going to begin the march without feeding the prisoners. The senior colonel said, "They will kill us all doing this, let's refuse to march unless we are fed." The Germans were furious and said, "You march, or else." Despite repeated threats, not one prisoner moved.

Soon a couple of big trucks backed up close to the prisoners, now lined up on the road. The tailgates were dropped revealing a manned heavy machine gun in each truck, pointed at the prisoners. A German officer repeated, "March, or else we will shoot." No one moved. This was repeated. No one moved. The Germans put the truck tailgates up, and fed the prisoners.

Jack Hemingway, son of Ernest Hemingway, in his 1986 book *Misadventures of a Flyfisherman*, identified the colonel as Paul (Pop) Goode.

****

Surviving combat means living the rest of your life with "what if" questions that have only one answer. What if I hadn't left my bunk to go to the head when the torpedo hit? What if I hadn't switched places with the crew chief the day ack-ack ripped the nose off my B-24? What if I hadn't turned my head a second before that bullet grazed my cheek?

I've sometimes asked myself, what if I hadn't gotten sick and had shipped off to Europe with the rest of my Basic Training cohort? It seems likely that I wouldn't have survived such a war. The fighting in Europe took place on a scale that dwarfed my war in the Pacific, both in terms of the numbers of soldiers and the calibers of the weapons. It was an industrial war where death dealing more often came from tanks, artillery pieces, and airplanes miles away. That war made a cynic out of Paul Fussell, an infantry lieutenant turned scholar, who became convinced that my father's virtues of "Caution and Cunning" were woefully outdated for modern warfare. (Fussell read and complimented my first book, which included some of my war story, and responded, "You are so right about the 'acting' stuff!") He quotes historian Geoffrey Perritt: "Perhaps there was a time when courage, daring, imagination, and intelligence were the hinges on which wars turned. No longer. The total wars of modern history give the decision to the side with the biggest factories."

I can't agree with this statement. My war in the

jungles against the Japanese left plenty of room for the qualities Perritt mentions. Far from an alienating experience, my service with a good, brave, and well-trained unit is my life highlight. It was a bloody war, but a good one. I learned much about the power of the human spirit and how individuals can function effectively through chaos, exhaustion, and fear. Perhaps I'd feel differently if my wounds had permanently maimed me and kept me from living an active life.

My positive feelings about the war probably explains my surprise when, on August 6, 1945, I heard over the loudspeaker at Nichols General Hospital that the atomic bomb had been dropped on Hiroshima. My immediate reaction was, "Why did they drop it on the women and kids?"

At that moment, I remembered having read well before Pearl Harbor "Lightning in the Night" by Fred Allhoff, a serialized story in *Liberty* magazine about a future World War in which atomic weapons were used. In the story, the United States was getting licked by the combined forces of Japan, Russia, and Germany until our scientists created an atomic bomb. We were able to convince Germany that we had the bomb, and they surrendered. But the Soviet Union refused to believe it, so we bombed them. Unlike Hiroshima and Nagasaki, this fictional drop was a demonstration on an unpopulated area. I believe the bomb blew a gigantic crater in the Russian steppes and killed nothing but some jack rabbits.

I remember thinking when I finished the story that the author Fred Allhoff had it about right. Americans wouldn't drop the first big bomb on non-combatants like women and children.

It surprised me that we did. If my infantry combat units had been asked whether the first bomb should be dropped on a purely military target or on a city like Hiroshima, I'm sure the vote would have been overwhelmingly in favor of sparing the women and children from the first bomb (though probably not the second). The vote might have been five or ten to one—even if we'd been told the U.S. had only two bombs. As young men in the infantry, we were largely idealistic about the war and against killing non-combatants.

But we were aggressive against the enemy. I was dismayed in 1947 when S.L.A. Marshall, a U.S. Army combat historian during the war, published a book arguing that only 25% of American soldiers in combat fired their weapons to injure or kill the enemy. "Fear of killing, rather than fear of being killed, was the most common cause of battle failure in the individual," Marshall wrote. "At the vital point, he becomes a conscientious objector."

Combat infantrymen spontaneously becoming

conscientious objectors on the battlefield? The notion was preposterous. My experience in combat was just the reverse. In a kill-or-be-killed situation, most of the men I knew lost any inhibitions against killing they may have had and fired their weapons effectively against the enemy. I took Marshall's contention as an unjustified put-down of warriors who did their duty and performed extremely well under fire. Indeed, their excellent soldiering won the war.

I might have forgotten Marshall's book, *Men Against Fire*, if its impact hadn't reverberated so profoundly in both military scholarship and tactics. The Army overhauled its training based on Marshall's findings in order to boost "ratios of fire," and many scholars have accepted his 25% figure (sometimes lowered to 15%) with little skepticism. All this, despite evidence that Marshall exaggerated his findings and fabricated many of his sources.

When I read Lieutenant Colonel Dave Grossman's *On Killing: The Psychological Cost of Learning to Kill in War and Society*—an otherwise excellent book that relies heavily on Marshall's mythical 25%—I decided to conduct a survey of holders of the Combat Infantry Badge. My hypothesis, tested informally through decades of conversations with hundreds of veterans, was that few CIB men would endorse Marshall's number.

Of the 150 questionnaires sent out by me and the Combat Infantry Association, sixty came back, forty from European Theater veterans and twenty from Pacific War veterans. Of the sixty who responded, thirty-seven agreed with the statement, "I positively believe I personally killed an enemy." More telling were their estimates of the percentage of non-firers. A full 90% of the respondents estimated that only 15% or fewer of their comrades didn't shoot to wound or kill. Over 70% of the respondents reported that between zero and 5% of soldiers failed to shoot to kill. These responses validated what I knew to be true from experience: us now old warriors used our weapons with great effectiveness against the enemy in World War II.

The side comments that these CIB holders wrote on their questionnaires were priceless. My favorite was by a Pacific War vet who said he'd run into only one guy, a replacement, who wouldn't shoot. This coward's excuse was that he "was too young to die." The vet's retort, delivered as he pulled the replacement out of his foxhole, was, "Me too."

****

I've returned to the Philippines four times since the war, the first time in 1964 when I traveled to Manila for business. I was only going to be there a few days, but I decided to try to locate the place where I'd suffered my final wound.

I hiked over six miles on a country road until I came to the gate of the Ipo Dam. I told the guard the purpose of my visit, and he showed me the scars on his shoulder from a gunshot wound he received while serving with the guerrillas. He took me to a fifteen foot high obelisk overlooking the dam. There was an inscription on a bronze plaque: "Erected by the 43d Infantry Division to the officers and men who fell in the Luzon Campaign, January 9-July 5, 1945."

I gazed at the dam, which I'd never seen during the fighting. Bright green water rushed over it in foamy white cascades. Considering the fury of the battle and the lives that were lost, I was disappointed in the dam's size. It stands only about thirty feet high and 200 feet wide.

I hiked alone down a narrow road which ended just above the dam and soaked my feet in the river. I sat in the humid quiet listening to the buzz of insects and enjoying the lush vegetation. Then, I climbed a steep foot trail to the ridge top, struggling though bamboo and twelve-foot-high cogan grass. After breaking out of the foliage, I spotted a tree stump about a quarter of a mile away. Stumps were rare in these grassy foothills, and it occurred to me suddenly that this was the location where my platoon had been. We'd been dug in on the reverse slope, and this low tree had stuck up above the ridge, marking the spot for the Japanese. Shells had hit the tree and exploded it, wounding several men in their foxholes. The men had used their bayonets to chop it down.

Walking over the slopes, I saw the old foxholes and even some bullet scarred helmets rusting in the tall grass. I was overcome by feelings of sad nostalgia, and my thoughts turned to Larry Daley, Hollis Morang, Bill Mitchell, Ed Barker and the other men who fought here. I took several photos, said a prayer for those who had died, and then started back down the hill, taking care not to step on an old mine.

On the foot trail, I came across a 75mm field piece, weighing over a ton, that the Japanese had dragged by hand. Evidence of tremendous determination and ingenuity, but for such a misguided purpose.

I returned also for the 50th and 60th anniversaries of the Luzon invasion, which the Filipinos celebrated in grand style. In January 1995, I met four-star General David A. Bramlett, a Vietnam combat veteran who was on hand to represent the United States in commemorating the Lingayen Gulf landings. We became instant friends. Fourteen Filipino ships and hundreds of troops performed a re-enactment of the landings with prodigious explosions. Some 20,000 spectators were on hand for the action.

In January 2005, I was the only American veteran of the Luzon campaign to return to the Philippines for the 60th anniversary ceremony. As a consequence, I was escorted to the stage and had my photo taken with various dignitaries, including former President Fidel Ramos.

The next day I roared in an open air tricycle cab to Pozorrubio to look for the rice paddy where Brammer and I had killed nine Japanese. I met with the town's mayor who sent me to examine an aerial photo of the town. I tramped about the rice paddies on the western boundary for six hours looking for the spot to no avail. The closest I got was probably 150 yards from the location. I returned to the town the next year and dedicated a monument to the exciting event that took place there in late January 1945.

Many probably wonder why I go to the trouble of making these trips back to Luzon. One of the reasons is the support we were given by the Filipinos in the war, and the fact that they are friendly toward Americans today. It's nice to be treated as a hero.

But a bigger reason comes from being a vet who enjoyed the good fortune of living out his child-

I've made four trips back to the Philippines since 1945. This is from the one I made in 2005, for the 60th anniversary of the Lingayen Gulf invasion. Here I pose with fellow WWII veteran Fidel Ramos, President of the Philippines, 1992-1998.

hood fantasies of combat. Americans kids of my generation grew up playing war games: cops and robbers, cowboys and Indians, Yanks and Germans. I remember digging a machine gun nest and trench in the back yard in second grade. We imagined shooting people, leading men, cracking jokes under fire, and winning battles against the nation's enemies. Then, many of us went on to do these very things at an impressionable age. The crucible of combat left its imprint on us and hastened our maturity. In some ways, I was more mature at twenty than I am at eighty-seven. It saddens me somewhat that I never again felt the sense of achievement that my Army career provided. I made mistakes in battle, but none that contributed to anyone's death. It was a good experience, and I have a natural desire to relive some of it on the ground where it happened.

****

I never cried during the war and never suffered from nightmares or other symptoms of Post-Traumatic Stress Disorder afterward. But in the summer of 1946, about three months after my discharge, I broke down briefly. I was driving to McHenry from Chicago with my dad in the passenger's seat. He had a good idea of what my war had been like not only because he was a veteran but because he'd read and saved the many letters I'd written to him while overseas (I wrote one every 3.4 days in service, including one every 4.9 days during Luzon combat and hospitalization on Biak).

We were listening to a radio drama about a veteran who'd been paralyzed by a bullet or shell fragment in the hips. It was a story akin to Fred

Zinnemann's 1950 film *The Men* starring Marlon Brando. Near the end of the program, the actor asks himself in a dramatic voice, "Was it worth it? Was it worth it?"

I pulled the car to the side of the road and sobbed uncontrollably. My dad, the old World War I stretcher-bearer, responded perfectly. He said nothing, but merely reached over and patted me lovingly on the back.

After a few minutes, I stopped crying. I pulled back on to the road, and the two of us continued home.

****

My eighty-seven years of luck has been heavily good, including being born into this wonderful country to great parents, given the honor of serving in the WWII army, and having a fine family and many other good friends. Infantry combat was the most enriching experience of my life, despite the fear, fatigue, frustration, wounds, sorrow and killing. Combat matured me rapidly, and since then I have rarely had as great a sense of doing something very necessary and worthwhile. Combat strengthened my Christian faith which remains strong. In combat I quickly learned the importance of communications, leaders, honesty, trust, humor and the power of emotions. In combat I became part of a band of brothers, and still think of the war every day. And I have been blessed with being able to talk with some combat buddies to this day.

To everyone who strives for good in the world, but especially the young, I urge them to remember the advice of a wise person, "Remember, the only thing necessary for the triumph of evil is for good people to do nothing."

APPENDIX ONE

Jay Gruenfeld's World War II Kills

Situation	Certain	Probable	50/50
1. January, Pozorrubio: Nine enemy with Chalmus Brammer at 10–40 feet. I shot first, second (grenade), and last, plus an unknown number of rest—body count.	3	2	1
2. January: Six small caves north of Mt. Alava, yielded eight bodies. Threw all grenades first five caves.	6	1	1
3. January: Sugarcane field. Eleven of us got ten. McAllister and I soloed one each. Eight of us got eight more in group shot. Range 10–50 yards.	1	1	1
4. January, other: Shots at no less than four individuals, 50–100 yards.	–	–	1
5. February, Antipolo, first patrol with new platoon. Put grenade in foxhole, 15–25 feet.	1	–	–
6. February: Four caves. I put grenade in two for ten body count. Group fired at eight. Nine suicides	1	1	–
7. March, Lovely Lady: Two shots to chest of enemy at 15–20 feet.	1	–	–
8. April: Enemy shot in coconut grove at 150 yards.	1	–	–
9. April: Twenty group fired at lone walker 100 yards.	–	–	–
10. May 14–15, Ipo Dam: Seventy shots at five individuals, ranges 100–500 yards. Hit magazine of 20mm gun. Missed lunch-eater eight times at 125 yards. Probable on skyline shot at 500 yards. ⎺	–	1	1
TOTAL	14	6	5

Jay Gruenfeld's Biography

Born: Nov. 24, 1924. Illinois

Military Service: Army of the United States, April 1943 to March 1946; overseas December 6, 1943 as buck sergeant to New Zealand. Served in Northern New Guinea campaign July-December 1944, 43d Division, 103d Infantry regiment, L Company, as staff sergeant, rifle squad leader, fourteen men. Made beachhead on Luzon, Philppines January 9, 1945. Received battlefield commission to 2d Lt. rifle platoon leader February 15, 1945. Was wounded five times (three minor), three Purple Hearts, last wounds May 15, 1945, near Ipo Dam, Luzon.

Education: B.S. Colorado State University (then Colorado A&M), March 1948; Master of Forestry, March 1949. Diploma from Oxford University, Dec. 1950, Politics, Philosophy and Forestry, Fulbright Scholar.

Employment History: Age 8 until going to college at age 16: Sold magazines door to door at age 8 to 10; age 10 until 16, part time work as golf caddy, then ran mid-course refreshment stand, McHenry, IL country club, various other minor jobs. Summer 1942: U.S. Forest Service, northern Idaho, pulled Ribes (plants that spread white pine blister rust) and fought fire. Summer 1947: U.S. Forest Service, redwood region California, gathering management plan field data. April 1949: began with Weyerhaeuser Company as a logging chokersetter, Longview, WA; after returning from Oxford graduate study, worked on logging railroad section gang, then scaled pre-logging timber falling; June 1951 to Monroe, WA as assistant forester, Skykomish Tree Farm, 55,000 acres. *I became forest manager (best job I ever had). When I took a promotion to the head office in 1957, we were managing 70,000 acres of age classes from zero to old-growth.* Left Weyerhaeuser in February 1969 after being Land Supervisor, Logging Superintendent, and corporate Manager of Timber and Log Sales. 1969-1972: Brooks-Scanlon, Bend, Oregon: Resource and Raw Material Manager for 200,000 acre ponderosa pine forest. 1973-1979: Potlatch Corporatioon, Vice President, Lands and Forestry, Lewiston, Idaho; 1.3 million acres Idaho, Arkansas, and Minnesota. 1980-1999: President, Jay Gruenfeld Associates, Inc. Seattle, WA; Forest Resource and Management Consultants. Worked in all regions of U.S., also Japan, New Zealand, Chile, and Russia. Published *Pacific Rim Wood Market Report* and gave thirty-seven conferences on Marketing Forest Products of the Pacific Rim, including four in Chile and one at Oxford.

Family: Jan, beloved second wife for thirty-six years, passed Sept. 2009; six children, eight grandchildren, five great grandchildren.

Other: Phi Kappa Phi, Xi Sigma Pi; Honor Alumni Colorado State U. and Honor Alumni, CSU College of Natural Resources; Honor Associate Alumni, U. of Idaho, College of Natural Resources; retired director of Pope Resources Corporation and Makah Forestry Enterprise; Fellow, Society of American Foresters, 1982; until recently an avid hunter, fisherman, and tennis player; Presbyterian. His first book, *Purple Hearts and Ancient Trees*, was published in 1997. He has a black Labrador Retriever named Riley.

Jay Gruenfeld
2071 McNeil St.
Dupont, WA 98327-8786

About the Authors

Jay Gruenfeld is a retired forestry executive and consultant who served as a rifle squad and platoon leader with the 43rd Infantry Division in the Pacific Theater in World War II. After the war, he studied in Oxford as a Fulbright Scholar and then became a forest resource expert specializing in the Pacific Rim. In 2002, he led the well-publicized campaign to have veterans visit and write the legendary combat cartoonist Bill Mauldin who lay dying in an Orange County nursing home. Jay has six children and lives in DuPont, Washington, where he enjoys big trees.

Todd DePastino is the award-winning author of *Bill Mauldin: A Life Up Front* (2008) and *Citizen Hobo: How a Century of Homelessness Shaped America* (2003). He is also editor of *The Road* by Jack London (2006), as well as *Willie & Joe: The WWII Years* (2008) and *Willie & Joe: Back Home* (2011). He is writing and co-producing the television documentary *Bill Mauldin's War*. He has a Ph.D in American History from Yale University and teaches at Waynesburg University. Todd lives in Pittsburgh with his wife and two daughters.